S0-ANN-399

TO YOUR HEALTH!
There's no antidote for laughter
with these medical jokes that are
sure to put you in a "hospitable"
mood. Whatever your ailment,
this treasure trove of outrageous
humor is the cure!

ON PSYCHIATRISTS
"I feel like a new man," the
schizophrenic patient said after
years of treatment. "Anyone I know?"
asked his doctor.

ON PHYSICIANS
"What can you give me for low blood
pressure?" Raymond asked. The
doctor handed him his bill.

ON DENTISTS
Why did the dentist have his office
windows removed?
He wanted to advertise himself as
paneless.

500 GREAT DOCTOR JOKES

500 GREAT DOCTOR JOKES

• ■ •

Jeff Rovin

A SIGNET BOOK

SIGNET
Published by the Penguin Group
Penguin Books USA Inc., 375 Hudson Street,
New York, New York 10014, U.S.A.
Penguin Books Ltd, 27 Wrights Lane,
London W8 5TZ, England
Penguin Books Australia Ltd, Ringwood,
Victoria, Australia
Penguin Books Canada Ltd, 10 Alcorn Avenue,
Toronto, Ontario, Canada M4V 3B2
Penguin Books (N.Z.) Ltd, 182–190 Wairau Road,
Auckland 10, New Zealand

Penguin Books Ltd, Registered Offices:
Harmondsworth, Middlesex, England

First published by Signet, an imprint of New American Library,
a division of Penguin Books USA Inc.

First Printing, May, 1993
10 9 8 7 6 5 4 3 2 1

 REGISTERED TRADEMARK—MARCA REGISTRADA

Printed in the United States of America

INTRODUCTION

Though the Greek physician Hippocrates didn't devise his code of medical ethics until around 400 B.C., doctor jokes are far, far older.

According to cave art found in Lascaux, France, the first human being to crack a medical joke was a shaggy brute named Ogg. It seems he saw another cave dweller fall into the river, and as the man struggled toward the bank Ogg shouted, "Hey, fellah! That's the worst case of water on the Neanderthal I've ever seen!"

The first joke about malpractice can also be traced to ancient times, to 30 B.C., when Cleopatra misread a physician's sloppy hieroglyphics and thought she was supposed to take an asp and call him in the morning.

Doctor jokes are still with us, and we've collected five hundred of them in this book—

some of them classics, many of them brand-new, all of them covering the medical spectrum from physicians to dentists to psychiatrists to specialists. (We've also included a final section about Big Mouth, a guy who could use two or three different doctors.)

Hopefully, this book will be just what the doctor ordered . . . a prescription for laughter.

DENTISTS

"I'm afraid I'm going to have to drill," the dentist told Gizelle.

"You mean," she said, "you can't do this without a rehearsal?"

• ■ •

Q: What's the difference between an orthodontist and a computer repair person?
A: One specializes in bites, the other in bytes.

• ■ •

"Hi," Marty said, "I'm calling to make an appointment with the dentist."

"I'm sorry, but the office is closed today."

"Good," said Marty. "When will it be closed again?"

• ■ •

Then there was the unhappy dentist who always looked down in the mouth . . .

• ■ •

. . . and the lovely young woman who didn't believe her dentist when he said he was out of gas . . .

• ■ •

. . . and the dentist who lobbied for stricter gum control.

• ■ •

"Your tooth is abscessed," the doctor said to Mr. Schneider. "I'm afraid I'll have to pull it."

"W-what'll that cost?"

"One hundred and fifty dollars—but it's got to come out."

"A hundred and fifty dollars," said Mr. Schneider. "Seems like a lot of money for two minutes of work."

The dentist shrugged. "If you'd like, I can pull it very, very slowly."

• ■ •

When the extraction was finished, Mr. Schneider said to the dentist, "Now, this may hurt a little. I can't pay the bill."

• ■ •

Q: What do you call someone who fixes teeth above the Mason-Dixon line?
A: A northodontist.

• ■ •

Q: What's the most expensive condition an orthodontist has to treat?
A: Buck teeth.

• ■ •

Mr. Horton phoned Dr. Estevez just before midnight.

"Sorry to call so late, but we've got a bit of an emergency here. You see, my son was kissing his girlfriend a while ago and—"

"Don't tell me," said Dr. Estevez, "locked braces."

"That's right," said Mr. Horton.

"I'll be right there, and don't worry—I have to unlock kids' braces all the time."

Mr. Horton said, "From an IUD?"

• ▮ •

Dr. Gish was heading out the door, golf bag slung over his shoulder, when the phone rang.

"It's Mr. Reynolds," said his assistant. "He says he has a cavity."

"Tell him to call back tomorrow," said the dentist. "I've got eighteen holes to fill this afternoon."

• ■ •

Q: Why did the dentist only see patients on his yacht?

A: He was an advocate of off-shore drilling.

• ■ •

Donna said to her friend, "My dad's teeth are all his own."

"You mean he finally finished paying for them?"

• ■ •

Then there was the dentist who had his office windows removed so he could advertise himself as paneless . . .

• ■ •

. . . and the lama who refused to take Novocaine because he wanted to transcend dental medication . . .

• ■ •

. . . and the dentist who was a baseball fan. During the day he yanked for the roots, and at night he'd do the opposite.

• ■ •

After having caps put on her teeth, the actress said, "That *really* hurt! I believe you are the worst dentist in the world!"

"No," said the dentist, "that would be too much of a coincidence."

• ■ •

Q: Why don't dentists eat much?
A: Because most of what they do is filling.

• ■ •

The dentist asked Rod, "And just how did you manage to lose all of your teeth in one night?"

"Beats the heck out of me," Rod said. "I fell asleep with my head under the pillow, and the next morning I had a mouth full of quarters!"

• ■ •

The dentist got home and, seeing his wife in tight shorts and a halter top, leaped on top of her.

As he slipped a hand beneath her waistband, she said, "Honey, please! You've had your hand in peoples' mouths all day!"

• ■ •

"I'm going to have to charge you three hundred dollars for pulling that tooth," the dentist told Jill.

"But why? I thought the fee was one hundred dollars."

"Normally, it is," said the doctor. "But your screams scared off my next two patients."

• ■ •

Q: What happened when the judge decided to practice dentistry on the side?
A: She believed in extracting the tooth, the whole tooth, and nothing but the tooth.

• ■ •

The dentist said to Mr. Pike, "There's good news and there's bad news. The good news is that your teeth are in great shape."

"And the bad news?"

"Your gums are so bad, they've all got to come out."

• ■ •

Q: What happened to the dentist who married the manicurist?

A: After a few weeks, they were fighting tooth and nail.

• ■ •

The dentist noticed the waitress's inflamed gums when she came to take his order.

"Pardon me," he said, "but I'm Dr. Silver. Do you have gingivitis?"

"I don't care who you are," the waitress said, "we only make what's on the menu."

• ■ •

Q: Why did the dentist's wife shoot him?

A: She heard about some of the cavities he was filling.

• ■ •

The bill for Hennesey's false teeth was way overdue, so Dr. Edwards decided to go to the old-age home and collect from the miserable old coot in person.

When he returned, the receptionist took one look at the dentist and said, "I take it from your expression that you didn't get your money."

"Not only didn't I get my money," said Dr. Edwards, "but the son of a bitch bit me with my own teeth!"

• ■ •

Q: What's the difference between a homeless man and a dentist?
A: One lives from hand to mouth, the other from mouth to hand.

• ■ •

Mrs. Falbo was shaking as she sat down in the dentist's chair.

"Dr. Wesson, I really hate coming to you to get my teeth filled. I think I'd rather have a baby."

"Well," said the dentist, "make up your mind so I'll know which way to adjust the chair."

• ■ •

Q: What's an orthodontist?
A: Someone who braces the kids but straps the parents.

• ■ •

Then there was the dentist's daughter who hung out with the worst set in town . . .

• ◢ •

. . . and the dentist who wanted a pull-time assistant . . .

• ■ •

. . . and the dentist who complimented the hockey player on his bright, even teeth: one, three, seven, nine, and eleven were missing.

• ▶ •

Q: What kind of choppers did the dentist make for the opera singer?
A: A falsetto teeth.

• ■ •

Millie sat down in the dentist's chair and promptly wrapped her hand around his testicles.

"What on *earth* are you doing?" the dentist asked.

Millie said, "We're not going to hurt each other, are we?"

• ■ •

"So," Wendy said to her husband, "how was the dentist?"

"A scream," he replied.

• ■ •

Drebin walked into the dentist's office with his wife.

"Listen, Dr. Sartwell," said Drebin, "there's a tooth I want pulled, but we're late for the opera. So skip the Novocaine and get to it."

"I admire your fortitude," the dentist said. "Which tooth is it?"

Drebin said, "Open up and show him, honey."

• ■ •

Finally, there was the dentist who bored his patients to tears . . .

• ■ •

. . . and the one whose patients drove him to extraction . . .

• ■ •

. . . and the dentist who was so lazy she swept her patients' tartar under their gums.

• ■ •

HOSPITALS

When the nurse came to give Mrs. Olsen her medicine, the patient looked askance at the pills.

"Excuse me, but I was just reading in a magazine about a woman who checked into the hospital because she had heart trouble—like me—and ended up dying because a nurse gave her the wrong medicine."

The nurse smiled. "Rest easy, Mrs. Olsen. When a woman comes in here with heart trouble, she *dies* of heart trouble."

• ■ •

Q: When do ten and ten equal twenty-six?
A: When you add ten ill people to a ward with ten ill people.

• ■ •

A voluptuous young woman was lying in bed, waiting to be wheeled to the operating room for breast-reduction surgery. Suddenly, a man in a white coat entered the room, lifted up the sheet, examined her breasts, then left. A minute later, another man in a white coat came in, felt her left breast, then her right, and headed for the door.

Confused and more than a little disgusted, the woman called after him. "I don't understand this. Aren't you ready to operate yet?"

"Haven't the foggiest," said the man in the white coat. "We're here to paint the room next door."

● ■ ●

The doctor took a week off and went hunting in Maine. When he got back to the hospital, a nurse asked, "How was your trip?"

"I didn't kill a thing," he complained.

"Hmph!" she said. "You'd have been better off staying here."

● ■ ●

"My father's been in the hospital for a month," little Ivy told her teacher.

"I'm sorry to hear that," the teacher said. "What's wrong?"

"Nothing," said Ivy. "He just became a doctor."

• ■ •

Fawn walked up to the floor nurse. "I'm here to see my friend Jake."

"Oh, you mean the man who had the dynamite accident?"

"That's the one," said Fawn.

"He's in room 211 . . . and 212, and 213."

• ■ •

Then there was the intern who quit the hospital to join the army and was enlisted as a semiprivate . . .

• ■ •

. . . and the hospital that was so crowded it couldn't accommodate a patient with double pneumonia . . .

• ■ •

. . . and the woman who was run-down and wound up in a hospital.

Q: Why didn't the hospital patient have a temperature in the afternoon?
A: Because the nurse took it in the morning.

Dr. Wainwright walked into the young woman's room.

"Good morning, Ms. Tish. Would you mind disrobing for me?"

"But Dr. Carlton just examined me thoroughly and said I was in absolutely perfect shape."

"Yes," said Dr. Wainwright, "he told me."

Gerard had just picked up Carla for their first date. As they were pulling away from her apartment building, Carla said, "I once had breast-reduction surgery. Want to see where?"

Nearly losing control of the car, Gerard said, "Yeah, sure!"

She pointed out the hospital as they drove past.

"Sorry to bother you," Rocky said to the nurse, "but can I please have another glass of water?"

"This is your twentieth glass!" she exclaimed.

"So it is," he said. "You see, my room is on fire."

• ■ •

Q: Does a sick ship ever go to the hospital?

A: No, just to the doc.

• ■ •

"We have a choice of meals today," the nurse said to her patient. "Steak or veal, take your pick."

"Thanks," he said, "but wouldn't a jack-hammer be more effective?"

• ■ •

Then there was the horny patient who asked to see the head nurse . . .

• ■ •

. . . and the doctor who passed a nurse

as he entered a ward. He cauterize and smiled. She intern smiled back.

• ◼ •

Heinrich was in the hospital with stomach problems, and he didn't feel like eating. He didn't even touch the broth they brought him for lunch, dinner, or before he went to bed.

The next morning, he woke up to an enema and a phone call from his sister.

"How are things going?" she asked.

"Not bad," Heinrich said, "but Ilsa, let me tell you something. If you're ever in here, make sure you eat the soup no matter *how* sick you feel. Otherwise, they wake you and shove it up your ass!"

• ◼ •

Lying in the emergency room, Zoey gasped, "Help me! I fell like I'm at death's door!"

"Don't worry," said the doctor, "we'll pull you through!"

• ◼ •

"I'll bet your wife misses you a great deal," the nurse said to Zeke.

"Nope," said Zeke. "I'm here 'cause her aim is excellent."

• ◼ •

When Mr. Hornsby was wheeled into the hospital with appendicitis, he was turned over to Dr. Swift—who, rumor had it, could perform the operation faster than any doctor in the state.

The surgery took place in a small amphitheater, and when word spread that Dr. Swift was in action, the place filled quickly with spectators. Incredibly, the surgery was completed in under five minutes.

An hour later, Mr. Hornsby regained consciousness in post-op. Much to his surprise, he was covered with bandages from his thighs to his chest.

When a nurse came by, Mr. Hornsby said, "Say, what happened here? Why do I need so many bandages for an appendectomy?"

"Well," the nurse said, "after Dr. Swift took out your appendix, the other doctors started to applaud and wouldn't stop."

"So?"

"So," she said, "he circumcised you for an encore."

• ◼ •

Dr. Kidd was alarmed to find a patient racing down the hospital corridor, holding his groin. A nurse was in hot pursuit, holding a still-steaming tea kettle.

After sizing up the situation, the physician screamed, "Hold on, Ms. Quirk! You weren't listening!"

The nurse stopped short. "What do you mean?"

Dr. Kidd said, "I told you to prick his boil!"

• ■ •

As he recovered, Mr. Durkee began making untoward remarks to the female doctors and pinching the bottoms of female nurses.

Finally, one of them got fed up with Durkee's behavior. "You know, sir," she said, "you don't belong in a hospital! You belong in a brothel!"

Durkee said, "At these prices, I could afford to be."

• ■ •

Rodney pulled up to the big man who was walking down a Pittsburgh street.

"Excuse me," said Rodney, "but what's the fastest way to get to the hospital?"

The big man said, "Say something rude about the Steelers."

• ▶ •

After putting Hector in a body cast, the emergency room doctor came over to get some information from him.

"What do you do for a living?" he asked.

"I used to be a window washer," said Hector.

"Used to be? When did you quit?"

Hector said, "About halfway down."

• ▶ •

Luther said to the nurse, "Do you think I could have an extra intravenous bottle today?"

"Why?"

"Well, I was thinking of asking someone to lunch."

• ▶ •

Greta was recovering from surgery, and the nurse brought her her dinner. The patient surveyed the plate.

"A piece of meat as thin as paper, a biscuit the size of a gumdrop, and a thimbleful of ice cream. You call that dinner?'

"I'm sorry," said the nurse, "but that's all I'm permitted to give you. Is there anything else I can get you?"

"Yes," said Greta. "A postage stamp."

"A postage stamp?"

"That's right. I like to read while I dine."

• ■ •

"Hi," the caller said to the nurse. "You have a patient on your floor—a Mr. Hipp. Can you tell me how he is?"

"He's doing fine," she said. "The doctor expects to remove the stitches tomorrow, and he'll be up and about within a week."

"Thanks," said the caller.

"Would you like me to tell Mr. Hipp you phoned?"

"This *is* Mr. Hipp," the caller said. "My doctor won't tell me anything!"

• ■ •

Frank said to Bill, "I hear your son swallowed a box of firecrackers."

"Yes, he did. He's in the hospital now."

"How's he doing?"

"So far, so good," Bill said, "but we haven't heard the last report."

• ■ •

Prudence went into her grandmother's room at the hospital.

"Good news, granny," Prudence said. "You're not going to need a hysterectomy after all."

"Thank goodness," she said. "And all because that nice priest came to visit yesterday."

"Uh, granny—that was a doctor."

"I see," she said. "I *thought* he was getting a little familiar for a man of the cloth."

• ◼ •

The doctor bumped into the elderly Mrs. Lumpkin and her walker as he hurried down the hospital corridor.

"Pardon me," said the physician.

"Oh my, yes," said Mrs. Lumpkin.

"Mine too," said the doctor, "but pardon me anyway."

• ◼ •

Mrs. Murdock came to visit her son Matthew in the children's ward.

"Mommy," he said as soon as he saw her, "I did a good deed today."

"What did you do?" she smiled.

"I put a tack on the head nurse's chair."

"You *didn't!*" Mrs. Murdock cried. "You said you did a *good* deed!"

"I did," Matthew protested. "All the kids in the ward hate her!"

• ■ •

Rockefeller was feverish and panting when he entered the emergency room. Certain he was going to die, the renowned skinflint said, "Doctor, I'll donate two million dollars to the hospital if you pull me through."

Working fast, the doctor determined that Rockefeller had food poisoning and treated him accordingly.

The next day, the doctor stopped by his patient's room to see how he was doing. Rockefeller was fine, and just before leaving the doctor said, "You know, Mr. Rockefeller, I'm going to hold you to your promise."

"What promise was that?"

"You said that if I pulled you through, you'd donate two million dollars to the hospital."

"I promised that?" Rockefeller said. "See? That shows you how sick I really was!"

• ■ •

The man ran into the emergency room and said to the first doctor he saw, "Quick! Do you know a cure for the worst case of hiccups in history?"

Without saying a word, the doctor drove a knee into the man's groin, forcing him to draw down a massive gulp of air.

"There," said the physician. "Bet you don't have the hiccups anymore."

"No," the man wheezed through his teeth, "but my wife in the car does."

• ■ •

"Yes," said one patient to another, "that's the modern hospital for you. TLC day after day."

"Yeah, tender loving care—"

"No," said the other patient. "Takes lotsa cash."

• ■ •

Q: What's the biggest difference between old and new hospitals?
A: In the old days, you got extensive care. Now it's just expensive.

• ■ •

Old Mr. Reed said to Mr. Richards, "Guess what? Last night I went out with a lovely nurse."

"Very nice," said Mr. Richards. "Now, if you could only control your bladder, maybe they'd let you go without one."

• ■ •

Dr. Nirenstein went to visit his sick patient Ellen in the hospital.

"I'm miserable," Ellen said. "All I want to do is get well and go back to work running my brokerage house."

Dr. Nirenstein said, "Why are you in such a rush? Don't you realize that you're better off than you were six months ago?"

Ellen's eyes widened. "Are you crazy? Six months ago I was buying and selling, hiring and firing, wheeling and dealing. Today, I'm lying here with a bleeding ulcer! How am I better off?"

Dr. Nirenstein said, "Six months ago you had dozens of problems. Today you have just one."

• ■ •

MEDICAL SCHOOL

The professor said to the class, "Today we're going to discuss the lungs and the heart."

A medical student leaned over and said to her neighbor, "Damn! Not another organ recital!"

• ■ •

Q: Why did the gambler enroll in medical school?
A: He heard there was a dice action class.

• ■ •

Then there was the student who flunked out after defining bacteria as the rear entrance to a cafeteria . . .

• ■ •

. . . and the farmer's son whose father worked hard to put him through medical school. As he said to his fellow students upon graduating, "All that I am I owe to udders."

• ■ •

Q: What's the difference between health insurance and a student doctor?
A: One's major medical, the other's the opposite.

• ■ •

The doctor was off teaching a class, so one of his new students answered the phone in his office. The call was from the school's football coach.

"Doc, it's Johnny Brown," said the coach. "He broke his arm in the fourth quarter."

"I see," said the aspiring doctor. "And, uh—exactly what part of the arm is that?"

• ■ •

"Why do you want to specialize in gynecology?" the professor asked young Robert.

The young medical student replied, "I hear there are lots of openings."

• ■ •

At the graduation ceremony, the dean of the medical school said, "Perhaps the most important advice I can give all of you is this: when you're not working, it's important for you to relax. But you can't relax if friends or acquaintances are always coming up and asking you for medical opinions. When that happens, there is one simple word which will put a stop to it."

The dean said, "Simply look the person in the eye and say, 'Undress.'"

• ■ •

The doctor slipped the X-ray onto the light box and turned to the medical student beside him.

"As you can see, one of the patient's legs is two inches shorter than the other due to a deformed fibula. This causes the patient to limp. Now, what would you do in a case like this?"

"Well, doctor," said the student, "I guess I'd limp too."

• ■ •

"Tetanus!" shouted the doctor upon entering the lecture hall. "Insulin! Booster!"

"What the heck is he doing?" one student asked another.

His neighbor replied, "Calling the shots."

● ■ ●

After leading the new medical students in prayer, the priest sat down and the doctor got up to welcome them.

"Your work as GPs will require you to diagnose most patients using two options," said the doctor. "Do they have a virus or not? If they have a virus, there are two options: will they get sick or not? If they do get sick, there are two options: will you save them or not?"

A student piped up, "And if the patient dies?"

The priest responded, "Then the patient still has two options."

● ■ ●

Hoping to increase his sexual staying-power for a hot date, the medical student snuck some pills which were supposed to increase the blood flow to his groin. Unfortunately, the medicine backfired and he ended up with hemorrhoids. . . .

● ■ ●

Then there was the stunningly hand-some and arrogant young medical student who, when taking the temperature of young women, automatically deducted ten degrees.

• ▪ •

NURSES

Tony walked up to the nurse.

"How's my brother doin'? He makin' any progress?"

"No," she said. "He isn't my type."

• ■ •

Tony stopped by his mother's house on the way home.

"How is your brother?" she asked.

"I think he's going to be there a long time," said Tony.

"Why?" she asked. "Did you see the doctor?"

"No," said Tony. "The nurses."

• ■ •

Q: What's the difference between a nurse and a beggar?

A: Nothing. They're both panhandlers.

• ■ •

Then there was the practical nurse who married a rich old man . . .

• ■ •

. . . and the nurse who always hummed sheet music when she tucked patients in.

• ■ •

"Nurse," said Isidore, "my feet are freezing. Would you mind getting me some socks?"

"I'm not allowed to do that," she said. "You see, I'm the head nurse."

"Fine," said Isidore. "Then please go and get me the foot nurse."

• ■ •

"You've got to help me," Hans told his doctor. "I feel like a nursedoo."

"What's a nursedoo?" the doctor asked.

"Takes care of the sick," Hans replied.

• ■ •

Then there was the obstetrician's harried nurse, who joined the longshoreman's union, claiming she was an abused doc worker.

• ■ •

Unfortunately, the nurse was fired when the doctor found out what she'd done. It marked the first time he'd ever turned his back on a woman who went into labor. . . .

• ■ •

Q: What did the nurse tell the doctor when Thomas Watt finally came out of his coma?
A: "Watt's up, doc!"

• ■ •

PHYSICIANS

Mr. and Mrs. Ogan were feeling rundown and went to the doctor.

After examining the middle-aged couple, the doctor said, "There's nothing wrong with you that a little exercise won't cure. Get out in the fresh air and work out. You should start seeing results almost immediately."

A month later, Mr. Ogan returned. "Doc," he said, "your suggestion was right on the money! I got myself some golf clubs and I've been hitting the ball regularly. I feel *great*."

"That's wonderful," said the doctor. "What about your wife?"

"Oh, I'm afraid there's no change. She absolutely refuses to exercise."

"Sorry to hear that," said the doctor. "I'd better have a talk with her."

"That'd be great," said Mr. Ogan. "I'd

hate to think I wasted over six hundred bucks on that lawn mower!"

•   ■   •

A few weeks after that, Mr. Ogan was talking to his neighbor, Mr. Pica.

"You look depressed," said Mr. Pica. "What's wrong?"

"My doctor just told me I should give up golf."

"Why? Did he look at your elbows?"

"No," said Ogan. "At my scorecard."

•   ■   •

"Doctor!" shouted the nurse. "You know that man to whom you *just* gave a clean bill of health? Well, he keeled over on the front step and died. What should I do?"

The doctor said, "Turn him around so it looks like he was walking in."

•   ■   •

"Dr. Pincus," said Mallory, "my hair's falling out. What can you give me to keep it in?"

The doctor said, "How about a shoebox?"

• ◼ •

"Would it hurt to play Ping-Pong on a full stomach?" Arthur asked his doctor.

"Well," the doctor replied, "I think a table would make more sense."

• ◼ •

"I hate it, I hate it, I *hate* it!" Felman wailed. "I can't *stand* having a cold."

"You'll just have to be patient," the doctor told him. "People get colds in the winter, and there's no cure—"

"But it's making me crazy. You've *got* to do something."

"Tell you what you can do," the doctor said. "Take a cold shower, wrap a towel around your waist, and run around outside the house for an hour."

"But doctor," said Felman, "then I'll get pneumonia."

"Yes, but *that* we have a cure for!"

• ◼ •

"So," Mr. Puckett asked his physician, "is it true that an apple a day keeps—"

• ◼ •

Q: Medicine for women is most effective when taken how?
A: In cider.

• ■ •

Mr. Elliot was changing a bulb when he banged his head on a beam and it began to ache something terrible. Since his wife wasn't home, he drove himself to the doctor. After examining it, the doctor told him that a hot compress would cause the pain to abate.

When Mrs. Elliot came home two hours later, she found her husband with a hot water bottle pressed to his head and asked what he was doing. He explained what had happened and what the doctor had told him.

Mrs. Elliot scoffed.

"Cold water is best for swelling," she said, and gave him an ice pack.

Within an hour the swelling had gone down and Mr. Elliot called the doctor.

"You know," he said, "you told me to use hot water on my head, my wife told me to use cold water, and she was right."

"What can I tell you," the doctor said. "My wife says hot water."

• ■ •

"Doctor," Isaac asked, "what's the best way to treat a mosquito bite?"

"You start from scratch," the doctor replied.

•　▪　•

Mrs. Merritt yelled, "Kyle, it's time for your medicine!"

"Okay, mom. I'll fill the bathtub."

"Why?"

"Didn't the doctor say I had to take it in water?"

•　▪　•

"Mr. Giguere," the nurse said over the phone, "the doctor is very upset. It's been two months since your visit and you haven't paid your bill."

Mr. Giguere replied, "Then tell him what he told me: take two aspirin and call me in the morning."

•　▪　•

"What can I do about my infernal sleep-walking?" Marci asked her physician.

The doctor said, "Spread thumbtacks on the floor."

• ■ •

The waiter walked over to Dr. Klein's table and said, "I have sauteed liver, frog's legs, and boiled tongue."

"That's nice," the doctor replied, "but I'm here to eat, not listen to your problems."

• ■ •

Q: Why did the dancer go to the doctor?
A: She had a ballet-ache.

• ■ •

Dr. Epstein and his wife were walking down the street when a stunning redhead in hot pants gave a little wave to the doctor.

"Who was that?" Mrs. Epstein asked.

"Oh, just someone I know professionally."

Mrs. Epstein asked, "Your profession or hers?"

• ■ •

Mrs. Snodgrass said to Mr. Snodgrass, "I've received a note from Dr. Benson about our party, but his writing is atrocious. I can't tell whether he's accepted our invitation or declined."

"Why don't you take it to the druggist," Mr. Snodgrass suggested. "Those people can always read doctors' writing."

Mrs. Snodgrass did as her husband suggested. The druggist looked at the writing, disappeared behind the counter, then returned a few minutes later with a small package.

"That'll be thirty-five dollars," he said.

• ■ •

Dimwitted Dennis went to see his doctor. "I want you to check my fingertips," he said.

The doctor looked puzzled. "Why your fingertips?"

"Because I don't feel well."

• ■ •

The medieval doctor's apprentice came running to his master's chamber.

"Sir," said the lad, "there's a wounded man at the door."

The doctor leapt out of bed and was shown to a warrior with an arrow in his belly. The physician pulled away the man's armor and worked to remove the shaft. But his mind was still clouded with sleep and his vision was hazy, and the bold soldier died.

Moral: never bother a doctor for anything in the middle of the knight.

• ■ •

Then there were the physicians who were Siamese twins, creating an eternal paradox . . .

• ■ •

. . . and the hypochondriac who never left the doctor's office well enough, alone . . .

• ■ •

. . . and the sword swallower who went to see his physician and was given a special diet: he was on pins and needles for weeks.

• ■ •

The woman rushed into the office. "Doctor, what's wrong with me?"

The man slipped his hands into the pockets of his tweed jacket and studied the woman. "For one thing, you're too fat. For another, you use way too much eye shadow. Also, your breath smells. And one more thing."

"What?" the stunned woman asked.

"You can't read. This is a bookstore."

• ■ •

The young woman phoned the doctor.

"It's my Uncle Oscar," she said. "He thinks he's sick."

"Ms. Belnick, I examined your uncle just the other day. I assure you, he's fine."

The next day, the woman phoned back.

"It's my uncle," she said.

"Let me guess. He still thinks he's sick."

"No. *Now* he thinks he's dead."

• ■ •

When Roseanne twisted her ankle, she debated about whether or not to go to the doctor; his fees, after all, were exorbitant. But she was in tremendous pain and, dragging herself to the car, she drove to his office.

"Fear not," said the doctor. "I'll have you walking before the day is out."

Sure enough, he did: he took her car as payment.

• ■ •

"I'm having difficulty breathing," Mr. Borland said to his doctor.

"I'll give you something to stop that," she promised.

• ■ •

The doctor said to not-bright Ned, "Be sure and take three teaspoonsful of this medicine after every meal."

"But Doc," said Ned, "I only have two teaspoons."

• ■ •

The doctor tried again. "I'll tell you what, Ned. I'll give you high-potency pills instead. Take one of them three times a day."

"Fine," Ned said, "but how can I take it more than once?"

• ■ •

The doctor tried one last time. "Okay, Ned—here's what you do. Go home, take a hot bath, open the medicine bottle, take a swig, then close it. You'll feel fine in a few days."

Ned went home. A few days later, the doctor called.

"How do you feel, Ned?"

"No better than when I saw you."

"Have you been taking baths?"

"Yes."

"And the medicine?"

"No."

"Why not?"

"Well," said Ned, "after I finish taking the bath I'm too darn *full* to take the medicine."

• ■ •

Maybelle yelled into the phone, "Doctor, what do I do? My baby fell down a well!"

"Go and get a copy of Dr. Spock's book."

"Dr. Spock? What good will *that* do?"

"What do you think?" the doctor asked. "It'll tell you how to raise baby."

• ■ •

"I'm afraid I'm losing my hourglass figure," the woman told her doctor.

"Then I recommend you diet."

"Really?" she said. "What color?"

● ◼ ●

Old Boswick went to see his doctor.

"How does it feel to be ninety?" the doctor asked his longtime patient.

"Not bad at all. And I attribute it to a ritual I adhere to religiously."

"Tell me about it. Maybe there's something I can pass along to my other patients."

Boswick said, "When I wake each morning, the housekeeper brings me black coffee and the newspaper. I drink my coffee while I read the newspaper."

"And then?"

"And then," said Boswick, "if I'm not in the obituary column, I get up."

● ◼ ●

Old Boswick and the doctor continued chatting during the examination.

"Tell me," said the doctor. "Do you ever think of the hereafter?"

"Constantly," Boswick replied. "Every time I open a drawer I stand there and think, 'Now what am I here after?' "

● ◼ ●

"I hear," the doctor said to Boswick, "that you're contemplating marriage to a twenty-two year old. Is that true?"

"It is," said Boswick, "though I've made it clear to her that my parents won't let me have relations as often as she might like."

"Your parents?" said the doctor.

"That's right," said Boswick. "Mother Nature and Father Time."

• ■ •

Q: What's the difference between seven days ago and a spine with slipped discs?

A: One's a week back, and so's the other.

• ■ •

Mr. Bakay walked into the doctor's office.

"Is that cough better today?" the doctor asked.

"Absolutely," said Bakay. "I practiced all night."

• ■ •

"Doctor, you've got to help me!" Michael cried. "This insomnia is driving me crazy!"

"Just sleep on the edge of the bed," replied the doctor.

"What'll that do?"

"You'll soon drop off."

• ◼ •

That still didn't help, so the doctor told Michael to try counting sheep. The next day, he phoned Michael.

"Did you do as I suggested?"

"I sure did."

"What happened?"

"I got up to 25,000."

"And then you fell asleep?"

"No," said Michael. "Then it was time to get up."

• ◼ •

"I don't get it," said Sam. "I can breathe all right during the day, but when I go to sleep I start gasping."

The doctor said, "Your problem is that you're breathing oxygen when you go to sleep."

"What *should* I be breathing?"

The doctor replied, "Nitrogen."

• ◼ •

Q: What did the doctor suggest to the man who was always regurgitating?

A: He told him to bolt down his food.

• ◼ •

Then there was the doctor who came down with the flu and got a taste of his own medicine . . .

• ■ •

. . . and the man who moaned so much when he was sick that his wife didn't know whether to call a doctor or a theater critic . . .

• ▣ •

. . . and the woman who fell down the steps and broke her jaw. Her husband waited two days before calling the doctor.

• ■ •

"Did you know that there are thousands of miles of blood vessels in your body?" the doctor asked his patient Larry.

"Phew!" said Larry. "No wonder people get tired blood."

• ▶ •

The doctor's intercom buzzed.
"Yes?"
"Doctor, the Invisible Man is here."
"Sorry, but I can't see him."

• ■ •

Walking over to where the artist was sprawled on the floor, the doctor lifted the canvas and heavy easel from her back and examined the inert painter.

After a moment, he rose and told the housekeeper, "I'm sorry to say she's dead."

"Wh-what happened?"

"I can't be sure," said the doctor, "but I'd say she suffered a stroke and then had an art attack."

• ■ •

As they sat in the expensive restaurant eating a rich dessert, Sammy said to his date Jessie, "If my doctor saw this he'd really be ticked off!"

"Why? Has he got you on a special diet?"

"No," said Sammy. "I owe him five hundred bucks."

• ■ •

Joseph was suffering from terrible headaches, so he went to see the doctor.

"Do you drink?" asked the doctor.

"Wouldn't touch the stuff."

"Smoke?"

"Vile. Never."

"What about sex?"

"It's a sin," said Joseph. "I don't even think about it."

The doctor put away Joseph's chart. "I think I know what your problem is."

"Really? What?"

The doctor said, "Your halo's too tight."

• ■ •

"How did you get here so quickly?" the doctor asked his patient.

"Flu."

• ■ •

Then there was the short-tempered doctor who was constantly losing his patients . . .

• ■ •

. . . and the man who saw several doctors about his brain, but they couldn't find anything . . .

• ■ •

. . . and the anemic chap who took a blood test and failed (a mosquito bit him, and all it got was practice) . . .

• ■ •

. . . and the patient who called his doctor an Indian giver, because first she said she'd treat him, and then she charged him.

• ■ •

Q: What's the difference between a crook and a pill to relieve PMS?
A: One's a pilferer, the other a pill for her.

• ■ •

Each and every day, the doctor stopped by the bar after his last appointment, and Wally the bartender always had the doctor's favorite walnut and rum drink ready and waiting. One day, however, Wally ran out of walnuts and was forced to substitute another nut.

The doctor came in as usual and, after taking a sip of the drink, made a face.

"Wally—this isn't my drink!"

Sheepishly, the bartender said, "It's something new."

"What *is* it?"

"Why—it's a hickory daiquiri, doc."

• ■ •

Q: What do you call someone with a sore
   throat and fleas?
A: Hoarse and buggy.

• ◄ •

Officer Winsted ran up to the prison war-
den. "Sir, a couple of prisoners have broken out—"
"Quick! Alert the local police and call out
the state troopers—"
"Maybe we ought to call the doctor first,"
Winsted said. "Looks like measles to me."

• ◼ •

"Do you suffer from arthritis?" the doctor asked her patient.
"Sure," said the patient. "What else do
you do with it?"

• ▲ •

"Sorry for the long wait," the doctor said
to Mr. Griswold.
"That's all right—though it probably
would have been better if you'd treated my
illness in its early stages."

• ◼ •

"Doctor," said Mel, "I've got potatoes growing out of my ears."

"That's odd."

"I'll say. I planted radishes."

• ■ •

"I just came from the doctor," Mrs. Abercrombie told her neighbor.

"Which doctor?"

"No," she said. "Internist."

• ■ •

Q: What did the woman say when she ran into the doctor's office?

A: "Ouch!"

• ■ •

Jerri got onto the crowded bus. As she stood in the aisle, she noticed a man sitting next to her, his head bent into his folded arms.

Jerri tapped him on the shoulder. "I'm a doctor. Are you feeling all right?"

The man looked up. "Quite all right. I just hate to see a woman stand while I sit."

• ■ •

The doctor told overweight Mr. Blandings, "The best thing you can do is stop drinking, cut out sweets, and give up potato chips."

Mr. Blandings said, "I don't deserve the best. What's second best?"

● ■ ●

The doctor was making conversation with his patient. "Do you know that some physicians claim marathon racing kills cold germs?"

"Really," said the patient. "I didn't know they made running shoes that small."

● ■ ●

Q: What's the best cure for water on the knee?
A: A tap on the leg.

● ■ ●

"I don't know what to do," Rhonda said to the doctor. "Each morning, I get up and I'm dizzy for the first hour."

The doctor said, "Have you tried getting up sixty minutes later?"

● ■ ●

"I don't get it," Oliver told his doctor. "When I stand on my head, all the blood rushes to it. Why doesn't that happen when I stand on my feet?"

The doctor said, "Your feet aren't empty."

• ■ •

"Dr. De Leon," said Rufus, "how can I live to be over a hundred years old?"

"Simple," said the doctor. "Just drink a glass of hot tea every morning for 62,400 weeks."

• ■ •

When little Ivan walked in the door with his mother, his sister asked, "What'd the doctor say was wrong with you?"

"Asthma."

The girl yelled, "Hey, ma! What's wrong with Ivan?"

• ■ •

David came home and said to his wife, Amy, "The doctor said I didn't break anything when I fell down the steps, though he did say I had a flucky."

His wife looked at him. "What's that?"

"I don't know," said David. "He said I was okay, so I didn't ask."

"Hold on. The doctor tells you you have something, and you don't ask what it is?"

"I didn't think it was important," David said.

Disgusted, Amy called the doctor and was put right through.

"Doctor," she said, "what's a flucky?"

There was a pause, and then he said, "I have no idea."

"But you told my husband he had one."

There was another pause. "No I didn't," said the doctor. "What I told him was, 'You got off lucky.'"

• ■ •

Q: What happened to the woman who discovered Chicago, IL?
A: She got in touch with Baltimore, MD.

• ■ •

Q: What city represents the greatest medical feat in history?
A: Lansing, Michigan.

• ■ •

An important call came to the Atlantic City hotel room of Dr. Vajna. Since the doctor was downstairs playing blackjack, his wife asked the manager to have him paged.

"I'm sorry," she was informed, "but the house does not make doctor calls."

• ■ •

"Doc," said the man, "I work like a horse, eat like a bird, and end each day tired as a dog. What do you recommend?"

The doctor replied, "A veterinarian."

• ■ •

Q: What are the most important things a doctor learns at medical school?
A: To write prescriptions illegibly and bills legibly.

• ■ •

"I've got good news and bad news," the doctor told Dexter over the phone. "The good news is that you've only got twenty-four hours to live."

"That's the *good* news?" Dexter said. "What could the *bad* news possibly be?"

"I've been trying to reach you since yesterday."

• ■ •

The hypochondriac said, "Doctor, I just *know* there's something wrong inside my brain."

"But the brain has no nerves. You wouldn't feel a thing, no pain of any sort."

"Yes, yes!" shouted the hypochondriac. "Those are *exactly* the symptoms!"

• ■ •

Sid was feeling terribly dizzy, nauseous, and light-headed, so he went to see his doctor.

"I hate to say it," said the physician, "but you may have an inoperable brain condition. You have, at the most, two months to live."

Determined to have fun during his last weeks on earth, Sid spent his every last dime on a fancy sports car and tailor-made clothes.

While he was being fitted for shirts, the tailor said, "Let's see . . . you've got a size sixteen-and-a-half neck—"

"No way," said Sid. "I wear a fourteen-and-a-half."

"Not according to my tape measure," said the tailor. "Why, if you tried to wear a fourteen-and-a-half neck, you'd feel dizzy, light-headed, and nauseous."

• ■ •

"Sorry I'm late for my appointment," Maurice told the doctor. "I tripped and sprained my leg."

"Of all the lame excuses!"

• ■ •

Q: What's the difference between a movie director and a doctor who sets broken bones?

A: Nothing. They both put people into casts.

• ■ •

"Dr. Arnold," said Charlotte, "what's the best way to avoid fallen arches?"

"Step around them," the doctor replied.

• ■ •

Dr. Warren met the nurse in the hall of the Balon mansion.

"What's that skinflint complaining about now?" the doctor asked.

"He's angry because he got well before the medicine ran out."

• ■ •

The doctor said, "To begin with, Mr. Jenkins, stand by the window, drop your pants, and bend over."

"What will that tell you?" Jenkins asked.

"Nothing," the doctor admitted, "but I really hate the doctor across the street."

• ■ •

Q: How long should doctors practice medicine?

A: Until they get it right.

• ■ •

"Mrs. Hegstrom," said the doctor, "in my opinion, you have acute meningitis."

"Thanks," she said, "but what's wrong with me?"

• ■ •

"Doctor," said Wayne, "I've been sick to my stomach ever since yesterday when I had oysters for dinner."

"Was the meat fresh?"

"Dunno," Wayne grimaced.

"Well, how did they look when you opened the shells?"

Wayne stared at him. "You're supposed to open the shells?"

• ■ •

"Dr. Dinsdale," said Margaret, "is it true I haven't very long to live?"

The physician thought for a moment. "Let's just say I wouldn't start watching any soap operas if I were you."

• ■ •

"So," the doctor said to his septuagenarian patient, "how do you find yourself these days?"

"Like always," said the woman. "I just throw back the covers each morning and there I am!"

• ■ •

"Doc," said Wes, "what do you suggest for flat feet?"

"Have you tried a foot pump?"

• ■ •

When the motorcyclist awoke, his physician was standing over him.

"Geez," said the biker. "Wh-what happened?"

"I've got some good news and some bad news, Chopper," the doctor said. "The bad news is, you've been in a terrible crack-up and I'm going to have to amputate your legs."

The biker rasped, "Christ! Wh-what's the g-good news?"

The doctor said, "See that guy in the bed next to yours? He wants to buy your boots."

• ■ •

"Doctor," Francine groaned, "I need something for my liver."

"Have you tried onions?"

• ■ •

Then there was the man who got a bad liver from being a bad liver . . .

• ■ •

"What's the surest way to cure a headache?" Mr. Hemsley asked the doctor.

"Just put your head through a window and the pane will disappear."

• ■ •

"I've been constipated for weeks," said Mrs. Shaw.

"What are you doing for it?" her doctor asked.

"Well, I'm sitting on the toilet an hour a day—"

"No, I mean what do you take?"

"Oh," Mrs. Shaw said. "I take my knitting."

• ■ •

The patient woke up with tire tracks across his chest and a doctor bending over him.

"Wh-what happened?" he asked.

"You're just a little run down," the doctor said.

• ■ •

After the doctor told her her brother Amos was dying, Sapphire went into his bedroom to see him.

"I—I'm going to see the lord," Amos said. "But before I go, can I have a piece of that delicious chocolate cake I smell?"

"Certainly not," Sapphire said. "I'm baking that for your funeral."

• ■ •

The doctor said to his balding patient, "I'm afraid there's nothing I can do to save your hair. The best I can do is shrink your head so it'll fit the hair you've got left."

• ■ •

Mary said to Jane, "Do you mean to tell me your big-shot doctor fiancé asked you to give back the ring?"

"Yes," said Jane. "Not only that, but he sent me a bill for thirty-six house calls."

• ■ •

"Doc," asked Murray, "what's good for a splitting headache?"

The doctor replied, "Glue."

• ■ •

Harry asked the doctor, "Is there any way I can live to be a hundred?"

"To start with," said the doctor, "you can give up sex. It puts a strain on the heart."

"Is that it?"

"No. Stop eating sugar. It causes your heart to race."

"Is that it?"

"Don't go to the movies or other crowded places. That'll lessen your chance of catching a disease."

"Is *that* it? Will I live to be a hundred?"

"No," the doctor admitted, "but it'll sure *feel* like it."

• ■ •

"Doc," said Seamus, "I keep seeing leprechauns whenever I open my eyes."

"That *is* a problem," said the doctor. "Have you seen a psychiatrist?"

"No," said Seamus. "Just leprechauns."

• ■ •

"The best thing you can do for your heart," the doctor said to Otto, "is walk five miles a week."

"I'll do it," said Otto.

"Great. How about caddying for me tomorrow?"

• ■ •

"What can you give me for low blood pressure?" Raymond asked.

The doctor handed him his bill.

• ■ •

"What's the best way to avoid diseases caused by biting dogs?" Simon asked the doctor.

The doctor said, "Don't bite any."

• ■ •

"Doctor," said Randall, "are oranges healthful?"

"I've never had to treat one."

• ■ •

The woman broke from her lover's passionate kiss. "You know, what I'm doing here is against doctor's orders."

"What's wrong?" asked the man. "You have a heart problem or something?"

"No," she said. "I'm married to one."

• ■ •

Q: How can you tell if a doctor is really a life saver?

A: By the hole in his head.

• ■ •

The salesman lay dying. "Son," he said, "go and call the funeral home."

"You mean the doctor, dad—"

"No," he said, "the funeral home. No point involving a middle man."

• ■ •

"Don't worry," the doctor told Renkin. "Your pulse is as steady as a clock."

"That's because you've got your hand on my wristwatch."

• ■ •

"Is there a sure way to tell mushrooms from toadstools?" Percy asked the doctor.

"Yes. Eat one before you go to bed. If you wake up the next morning, it's a mushroom."

• ■ •

"I don't like the looks of your wife," the doctor told Mr. Lipes.

"Me neither," said the man, "but she's a hell of a cook."

• ■ •

The medical student said, "Dr. Richardson—what's the deadliest poison of all?"

"Aviation," the doctor replied. "One drop and it's all over."

• ■ •

The Texan was driving through Maine when he pulled up to a gas station.

"Where can I find a doctor?" he asked.

"Why?" said the New Englander. "You feelin' ill?"

"Just a little claustrophobic," said the Texan.

• ■ •

The doctor walked into the office. "What's that you're taking, Rachel? The pill?"

"No," she said. "Valium. I forgot to take my pill."

• ■ •

Mr. Howitzer went to the doctor and learned that he had only ten hours to live.

Rushing home, he told his wife.

"Honey," she said, "let's go to bed. I'm going to make this the most memorable ten hours of your life."

Once they were undressed, the woman did everything that he'd ever wanted a woman to do.

When they were finished, Mr. Howitzer asked her to do it again. She knew it would take a great deal of strength and determination, but she obliged.

When they were finished, it was three in the morning and the woman was spent. As she lay flat on her back, her husband asked her for one more session.

Looking him square in the eye, she said, "Sure—what do you care? *You* don't have to get up in the morning!"

• ■ •

Q: What do you call a bloodhound who's an EMT?
A: A medical scenter.

• ■ •

Nancy took off her clothes and sat on the examining table. The doctor put a hand on her shapely throat.

"What do you think I'm doing?" he asked.

"Examining my thyroid," she said.

Smiling, the doctor, began rubbing her bare breasts.

"What am I doing now?"

"Checking for lumps," she said.

Unable to contain himself, the doctor pulled down his pants and threw himself on top of her.

"What am I doing now?" he asked in the heat of passion.

Nancy said, "Examining the herpes I came here to have treated."

• ■ •

"I don't know," Carl said to his doctor. "That hair restorer you recommended doesn't seem to be doing me any good."

"Really?" said the doctor. "It's done me a world of good."

"You mean you've got new hair?"

"No," said the doctor, "a new BMW. I invented the stuff."

• ■ •

"What should I do about my son?" Marge asked the doctor. "He's got the flu and the thermometer keeps dropping."

"One thing at a time," the doctor said. "First, put the thermometer where he can't reach it. . . ."

• ■ •

"Doctor," said Betsy, "would you give me something for my head?"

"What would I do with it?" the doctor asked.

• ■ •

Q: What's the difference between an itch and an allergy?
A: A fifty-dollar office visit.

• ■ •

The woman went to the doctor and said, "You've got to give me something to keep my husband awake. Every time we make love, he falls asleep with his erect member still inside of me."

"That's not terribly unusual," the doctor said.

"Maybe not," said the woman, "but my husband sleepwalks."

• ■ •

Then there was the doctor who gave his patient two months to live. When the woman said she wouldn't be able to pay the bill, he gave her two more months.

• ■ •

During a dinner party, a man to the left of Dr. Thorkel kept telling him about ailments he had and asking what the doctor thought. When the man excused himself to go to the rest room, Thorkel turned to the woman on his right.

"How annoying!" the doctor said. "What do you think—should I charge him sixty dollars for a professional consultation?"

"Absolutely," said the woman. "By the way—that will be seventy-five dollars. I'm a lawyer."

• ■ •

"I'm really concerned," Loree said to the doctor. "Ever since you told me to use a diaphragm, I've been urinating purple."

"That's strange. What kind of jelly are you using?"

Loree said, "Grape."

• ■ •

Ripley was having terrible headaches, so he called the doctor for an appointment.

"I can squeeze you in next week," the office assistant told him.

"Next week? Lady, I could be *dead* by then."

"In that case," she said, "please have someone call and cancel the appointment."

• ■ •

Mrs. Foster said, "Doctor, I'm in such pain I just want to die!"

The doctor said, "You did the right thing coming to me."

• ■ •

Dr. Kelsey was walking down the street when she saw a man swerve to avoid hitting a dog. His car plowed into a telephone pole, and his head hit the dashboard.

Rushing over, Dr. Kelsey pulled open the door, undid his seatbelt, and bundled her coat beneath his head.

"Are you comfortable?" she asked.

The man said, "I make a good living."

• ■ •

"I really need help," Mort said to the doctor. "Every day, without fail, I move my bowels at eight A.M. sharp."

"What's wrong with that?"

Mort said, "I don't get up until nine."

• ■ •

Dumb Grimsdyke came home and found a man in bed with his wife.

"Okay, buster," said Grimsdyke, reaching for a golf club, "prepare to get clobbered."

"Wait!" said Mrs. Grimsdyke. "Th-this man is a doctor. He's taking my temperature."

"Your temperature," Grimsdyke said, tightening his grip on the club. "Okay. But when that thing comes out, it damn well better have numbers on it!"

• ■ •

"I'm here because of a very serious problem," lovely Leslie said to her doctor. "Every time I sneeze, I have an uncontrollable urge to make love."

"I see," said the doctor, who left the examination room and returned a few minutes later with a small container.

"I want you to try this," he said.

"What is it?"

The doctor replied, "Pepper."

• ■ •

"This bill is much too high!" Mrs. Thompson complained to the doctor.

"You forget, Mrs. Thompson, I saw Billy four times when he had the chicken pox!"

"And you forget how much you made when he gave it to the rest of the third grade!"

• ■ •

The receptionist called one of the doctor's patients.

"Mr. McGraw, the check you gave us for your office visit came back."

"Then we're even," said McGraw. "So did my headaches."

• ■ •

Q: What do a cold and a town meeting have in common?

A: Sometimes the eyes have it, other times the nose.

• ■ •

Nolan said to a friend, "My ancestors followed the medical profession."

"Really? They were all doctors?"

"Nope. Undertakers."

• ■ •

Manfred asked, "Doctor, what's your favorite sport?"

"Sleighing."

"No," said Manfred. "I mean apart from your profession."

• ■ •

Prudish Mrs. Fiala went up to the doctor at the wedding.

"I—I understand my daughter spoke to you about s-e-x," she said.

"She most certainly did. She asked if I thought it was all right for her to have relations before she was married."

Blushing, Mrs. Fiala said, "What did you tell her?"

"I said I saw nothing wrong with that as long as it didn't hold up the ceremony."

• ■ •

Dr. Baxter was arguing with his patient Phyllis, with whom he was having an affair.

"And another thing!" he yelled as she stalked toward the door. "You're one god-awful lay!"

Phyllis left, and, after cooling down, the doctor decided to drive out and apologize to Phyllis. When he walked into her house, he saw her in the arms of another man, a physician with whom he was acquainted.

"What the hell are you doing?" Dr. Baxter cried out.

"What does it look like?" Phyllis replied. "I'm getting a second opinion."

• ■ •

It was well after midnight and there was a knock on the doctor's door. Dragging himself to the window, he looked down at a man in a bathrobe.

"Well?" snapped the doctor.

"No," said the caller. "Sick."

• ■ •

"My husband just doesn't show the sexual energy he had during our youth," the woman complained to her doctor.

"I see. And how old is your husband?"

"Seventy-five."

"Well, you can't blame him, can you? Tell me—when did you first notice that there was a problem?"

"Last night," she said, "and then again this morning."

• ■ •

"I've got a sexual problem," doltish Donald said to the doctor. "Every time I get it in part of the way, my eyesight gets blurry. And when I get it in all the way, I get blind as a bat."

"Very curious," the doctor agreed. "Please let me see it."

Donald stuck out his tongue.

• ■ •

Then there was the doctor who enjoyed bad health . . .

• ■ •

. . . the physician who pointed out that the only negative side effect of many medicines is bankruptcy . . .

• ■ •

. . . and the man who got upset when the doctor handed him his bill. In fact, he was so distraught that the physician had to charge him an extra ten dollars for a sedative.

• ■ •

Seamus was washing windows when a sudden gust of wind carried him off the scaffold. Arms akimbo, he plunged two stories to the street, where, as fate would have it, he landed at the feet of a doctor.

"Don't move," the physician told him. He told one passerby to call an ambulance, and asked another to get him a drink of water.

"Mother Mary," Seamus said. "How far does a man have to fall to get a shot of liquor?"

• ■ •

After three visits, the doctor was unable to cure Saul's constipation. Looking for a clue as to what might be causing it, the doctor asked, "What line of work are you in?"

"I'm an actor."

The doctor pressed a ten dollar bill into the man's hand, and Saul looked at it.

"How's that going to cure me?"

The doctor said, "Go and eat something."

• ■ •

Q: What's the difference between a sociable doctor and a bad doctor?

A: Nothing. Both have patients who tend to drop over.

• ■ •

"I don't understand why my little Sheppy Jebby is losing weight," his mother said to the doctor. "He gets plenty of exercise, sunshine, and sleep."

"What does he eat?"

The woman frowned. "Damn! I *knew* we were forgetting something!"

• ■ •

"I'm very concerned about my son's health," Mrs. Dean said to the doctor.

"Why? What does he have?"

The woman said, "A Porsche."

• ■ •

When Peterson arrived for work, his secretary said, "Gee, Mr. P.—you look terrible."

"I do? That's strange, because I feel really great."

Peterson put her comment from his mind until his boss walked into the office.

"Peterson—you feeling okay? You look terrible."

"So I've heard. But I feel really great."

Concerned, Peterson made an appointment to see his doctor during lunch. The instant he walked into the examination room, the doctor said, "Mr. Peterson—you look terrible."

"I *know*!" he said. "All day long everyone's been telling me that, but I feel *great*!"

After a full physical, the doctor couldn't find anything wrong with Peterson. However, he decided to check his big book of symptoms before pronouncing the man to be in good health.

"Looks terrible, feels great," the doctor

muttered, flipping through the pages. "Looks terrible, feels great—aha! I've got it. Mr. Peterson: you're a Vagina."

• ■ •

Q: What's the difference between a doctor and a germ?
A: The germs don't attack your checkbook.

• ■ •

The woman went to the doctor complaining of pain in her neck and knees.

"Is there anything you do on your knees?" the doctor asked. "You know, like scrubbing the floor?"

"Well, my husband and I always have sex in that position."

"I see. You know, there *are* other positions you can assume to have intercourse."

"Not if you want to watch TV there aren't."

• ■ •

Then there was the hypochondriac's hypochondriac who wanted to be buried next to a doctor . . .

· ■ ·

. . . and the doctor who told his patient she was not sick because of what she was eating, but because of what was eating her . . .

· ■ ·

Q: What's the difference between youth and old age?
A: Old age is when most of the names in your little black book are doctors.

· ■ ·

Ethel called her doctor and asked, "What can I take for laryngitis?"

"Sorry, I can't hear you."

"Laryngitis."

"I still can't hear you."

"My pipes!" she rasped.

"Sorry?"

"My *pipes*! You know—what runs from the kitchen to the bathroom!"

The doctor said, "You got cockroaches, call an exterminator!"

· ■ ·

Q: What's the difference between acupuncture and traditional medicine?
A: Very little. With one you get stuck with needles, with the other, a bill.

● ■ ●

Stefan cried into the phone, "Doctor, I just dropped twelve stories and I think I broke my toe."

"You're lucky that's *all* that happened!"

"Well," Stefan said, "it wasn't a very heavy anthology."

● ■ ●

Later, Stefan called back and said, "Doctor, I just fell off a thirty-five foot ladder and I think I broke another toe!"

"Migosh," said the doctor, "you're lucky that's all that happened."

"Not really," said Stefan. "I was only on the second rung."

● ■ ●

"I need your help," Mr. Grieg said to the doctor. "Every ten minutes, a man is hit by a car in this city."

"Why is that your problem?" the doctor asked.

"Because I'm that man."

• ■ •

"What should I do?" Mrs. Benet said to the doctor. "My son Billy was just stung by a wasp."

"Try putting cold cream on it."

"I can't," she said. "It flew away."

• ■ •

"I'm here because of my husband," the woman told her doctor. "Whenever we're having sex, he climaxes with an incredible yell."

"That's hardly unusual. In fact, many women find that exciting."

"And I would too," the woman said, "if it didn't keep waking me up."

• ■ •

Mr. Martin said to Mr. Fonebone, "The doctor sent my daughter to Arizona for her sinuses."

"Of course," said Mr. Fonebone. "Why should he go and get them?"

• ■ •

Then there was the doctor who described his patient's asthma as "the summer disease," since his breath came in short pants . . .

• ■ •

. . . and the man who complained that at today's prices, *any* pill was a bitter one to swallow.

• ■ •

Little Tommy said to little Albert, "A little chicken just came by and told me what kind of a man your dad is."

"Yeah? What kind?"

Tommy said, "Cheep, cheep."

Albert lifted his chin and said, "Guess what? A little duck just came by and told me what kind of doctor your dad is."

• ■ •

The pride of Poland, Dr. Zarchowski, happened to be dining in an Italian restaurant when two waiters opened fire on a well-dressed man sitting at the table beside him.

When the smoke cleared, Zarchowski saw the bullet-ridden body and ran over.

"How is he?" asked one of the fallen man's dinner companions.

"Thank God," Zarchowski said. "Except for the bullet that stopped his heart, these other five aren't too serious."

• ■ •

The doctor said to Pete, "I'll examine you for sixty dollars."

"It's a deal," said Pete. "And if you find it, you can keep half."

• ■ •

"My wife is in a real sorry state," the man told his doctor. "She usually stays awake till two or three in the morning. What can I do for her?"

"Come home earlier," the doctor advised.

• ■ •

The woman was sitting in the examination room when the lab technician walked in.

"Mrs. Shapiro, this isn't a urine sample you gave me. It's apple juice."

The woman bolted from the table. "Out of my way! I've got to call my son's school!"

• ▦ •

The doctor told Mrs. Ziegler, "If you still have a headache this afternoon, do what it says on the aspirin bottle."

"Take two every four hours?" she said.

"No," the doctor replied. "Keep away from children."

• ▦ •

The medical group was honoring a retiring member, Dr. Falk, who happened to weigh nearly three hundred pounds.

No sooner had Dr. Falk stepped to the podium than one side of the dais collapsed. As the distinguished panel struggled to their feet, one of them looked up from the sloping platform and cried, "Is there a carpenter in the house?"

• ▦ •

Dr. Mix and Dr. Thomas met for their very competitive Wednesday golf game. As they set out, Thomas asked Mix, "Where's Dr. Sanchez?"

"Didn't you hear? His wife wouldn't let him play on Saturday so he picked up a golf club and beat her to death."

"Geez," said Dr. Thomas. The two men were silent for a moment, after which Thomas asked, "How many strokes?"

• ■ •

Then there was the doctor who just couldn't understand why Americans spend ten times more on get-well cards than on medical research. . . .

• ■ •

The stage actor went to the doctor, unable to shake the flu he'd had for over a week.

"I'm so *sick*," said the actor. "I feel as though titans are clashing in my head, the sparks from their swords liquefying the contents of my nose. You must do something for me, heir of Hippocrates."

The doctor wrote out a prescription and handed it to the actor.

"Sugar?" said the actor. "What will this do?"

"Plenty," said the doctor. "Haven't you ever heard of sugar-cured ham?"

• ■ •

As Dr. Goldblatt examined Mrs. Michaelson, he listened to her tell him about her ailments, and then about her grandchildren.

When he was finished with the examination, he asked her to stick out her tongue for five minutes while he sat at his desk, writing. When he was through, he handed her a slip of paper.

"That was excellent. Now take the pills I've prescribed and you'll be fine in a day or two."

When Mrs. Michaelson left, his nurse came over and asked, "Why did you have her stick out her tongue like that?"

"It was the only way to shut her up while I figured out what to give her."

• ■ •

Mr. Christian was shaving one morning when he dropped the can of shaving cream on the toilet seat, scratching it.

Knowing how particular his wife was

about her bathroom, he quietly slipped downstairs, found paint that was just the right color, and repainted the seat.

Now he was late for work and, running out the door, forgot to leave his wife a note about the toilet seat. When she got up and went to the bathroom, Mrs. Christian found herself stuck fast to the seat.

Unable to budge, she sat there sobbing until her husband came home. When he saw what had happened, he begged her forgiveness, then unbolted the seat, helped his wife to the bed, lay her on her belly, and phoned Mr. Clark, the emergency medical technician who lived down the street.

When Mr. Clark arrived, Mr. Christian showed him to the bedroom and pointed to his wife's buttocks, which was stuck in the toilet seat.

"Well?" said Mr. Christian. "What do you think?"

Mr. Clark said, "It's really nice, but why'd you get such a cheap frame?"

• ■ •

As the doctor was finishing up Roy's examination, he noticed the man's shins were badly bruised.

"What's that from?" the doctor asked. "Football? Soccer?"

"Nope," said Roy. "Bridge."

• ■ •

Moe, Larry, and Carly were sitting in a rowboat talking.

Moe asked the others, "What would you do if your doctor told you that you only had a month to live?"

"Well," said Larry, "I'd use my life savings to take a trip around the world."

"And you?" Moe asked Carly.

"I'd hire the Cincinnati Pops to play all of my favorite orchestral music." She looked at Moe. "What would you do?"

"Me? I'd go see a different doctor."

• ■ •

The doctor came to the old age home to check on ninety-nine-year-old Mr. Mapes. Upon finishing the examination, the doctor said, "I fully expect to see you celebrate your one hundredth birthday."

"No reason why you shouldn't," said Mr. Mapes. "You look pretty healthy to me."

• ■ •

The drill sergeant went to the dispensary and asked the doctor for something to treat an awful, hacking cough.

"One thing you could do is give up cigarettes," the doctor said.

"Hey, I *did*," said the sergeant.

"When was that?"

"Nineteen fifty-eight."

"Impossible," said the doctor. "I can still smell smoke on you!"

"Well, what do you expect?" the sergeant shot back. "It's only twenty-two twenty-eight now."

• ■ •

The medical board had convened to decide what to do about Dr. Moriarty.

"What do you have to say for yourself?" one of the board members asked.

"Look," said Dr. Moriarty, "it's like this. I got up that morning and when I tried to shut the alarm, I broke my glasses. I stumbled over to the dresser to get my other pair and accidentally stepped on the cat. She clawed my foot and, hopping with pain, I tripped over the scale and cracked my head on the windowsill.

"When I finally managed to get dressed and out of the house, I had a fender bender on the way to the office. When I arrived, I was nearly an hour late. In my haste, I spilled hot coffee on myself, and then I had to deal with Mr. Price—who is easily the crankiest patient of all time.

"So," Dr. Moriarty concluded, "when my nurse came in and asked what she should do with the new shipment of thermometers, can you blame me for showing her?"

• ■ •

"I've got news for you," the doctor told his female patient. "Go home and tell your husband you're going to have a baby."

"But doctor, I'm not married."

"I see. Well then, go home and tell your lover."

"I don't have one," she said.

The doctor replied, "Then go home and have a seat by the door."

"Why?"

"Because three wise men should be showing up before long. . . ."

• ■ •

Bernard told Miles, "My doctor said that if I didn't stop chasing women, I'd be dead before very long."

"That's a strange thing for him to say."

"Not really. One of the women is his wife."

• ■ •

"You're gaining weight," the doctor told Mr. Koch.

"Is it that apparent?"

"Let me put it this way," the doctor said. "When I took out your appendix, the scar wasn't a foot long."

• ■ •

Then there was the doctor who got an alcoholic patient to give up drinking by convincing him that grapes were wine in pill form. . . .

• ■ •

Elizabeth went to see her Malibu doctor.

"How are you today?" the doctor asked.

"Terrible. I've got the worst sore throat in the world."

"You know what I find works surprisingly well? Sucking on a lifesaver."

"Maybe that's convenient for you," she said, "but I live miles from the beach."

• ■ •

Mrs. Hardy had a serious weight problem, so she went to see her doctor.

"I'll *never* lose weight," she said. "I like food too much."

"There's a trick to dieting," said the doctor, "and that is *not* to eliminate your favorite food. Now, what's yours?"

Mrs. Hardy thought for a moment, then answered. "Thirds."

• ■ •

Mrs. Hardy phoned her doctor after returning from two weeks at a fat farm.

"What did you lose?" he asked.

She answered, "Fourteen days."

• ■ •

The doctor asked Mr. Muns, "How's your arthritis?"

"Ah," said Muns, "I can't kick."

• ■ •

Mrs. Holly went to see Dr. Maudlin about her husband's seriously under-active libido. Since she didn't want to hurt her husband's feelings, she asked for something she could give him without his knowledge.

"Just put one of these pills in his food," the doctor said, "and you should see results immediately.

That night, she did as the doctor said, chopping up the pill and putting it in pasta sauce. Serving it to her husband in front of the TV, she returned to the kitchen and waited.

Suddenly, she heard a scream and ran in. Screaming herself when she saw what the problem was, she ran to the phone and called the doctor.

"What's the matter?" the physician asked. "Didn't you see any results?"

"Did I ever!" she said. "Now tell me—how do I get the spaghetti to lie down?"

• ■ •

Sixteen-year-old Fran went to the doctor to have an abortion.

"When did this happen?" he asked as he prepared the patient.

"When my parents were at the movies.

There was nothing to do, so the boy next door came over and—well, you know."

"Why didn't you go to the movies with your parents "

Fran said, "I couldn't. It was rated NC-17."

• ■ •

"Doc," said Graham, "what can I do about this ringing in my ears?"

The doctor said, "Have you considered an unlisted head?"

• ■ •

Then there was the man who went to the family doctor. As he put it, "He treats mine, and I support his."

• ■ •

A nurse sent a copy of the bill to Mr. Neuhaus, and wrote at the bottom, "This bill is one year old."

Mr. Neuhaus sent it back with a note of his own: "Happy birthday."

• ■ •

Then there was the doctor who rushed his first four patients to the hospital, before he realized his stethoscope was busted. . . .

• ■ •

Q: What does the army call a lavatory for a medic?
A: A doctrine.

• ■ •

Old Mrs. Porter said to her friend, "I went to the doctor and he told me skipping is a great way to lose weight."

"Skipping? At *your* age?"

"Sure," Mrs. Porter said. "Skipping lunch, skipping dinner, skipping snacks . . ."

• ■ •

Then there was the cynic who pointed out that doctors have the best of both worlds: they can boast about their successes and bury their failures. . . .

• ■ •

Q: What does a famed gunfighter have in common with the Fourth of July?
A: Both are Doc holidays.

Then there was the doctor who gave a drowning man mouth-to-mouth resuscitation, marking the first time a patient made a full recovery thanks to medic air. . . .

• ■ •

It was three in the morning, and the kleptomaniac screamed into the telephone, "Doc, you've got to help me! I'm in a hotel room and I've got my old urge to steal again!"

"You'll be fine," replied the doctor.

"But what do I do *now*?" he yelled.

"What do you think?" said the doctor. "Take two hangers and call me in the morning."

• ■ •

Mrs. Gold said to Mrs. Wachtel, "You know, you really ought to go see my doctor."

"Why? There's nothing wrong with me."

Mrs. Gold said, "He's so good, he'll *find* something."

• ■ •

"I can't do anything for your problem," the doctor told Mr. Clark. "It's hereditary."

"I see," said Clark. "In that case, send the bill to my grandfather."

• ■ •

PSYCHIATRISTS

"Doc," Jake said, "my wife thinks she's a rubber band!"

"Just tell her to snap out of it!"

• ■ •

"Why are you here?" the psychiatrist asked Mr. Kennedy.

"Because I like boxer shorts more than jockey shorts, and my wife thinks I'm crazy."

The doctor was stunned. "Why, I also prefer boxer shorts."

"You do?" Mr. Kennedy enthused. "How—with hot fudge or caramel sauce?"

• ■ •

"Doctor, I've got a terrible problem. Can you help me out?"

"Certainly," said the analyst. "Which way did you come in?"

• ■ •

The psychiatrist told his new patient, "Your problem is that you attach much too much importance to material things."

"Can you cure me of that?"

"I can indeed," said the analyst. "That'll be five hundred dollars."

• ■ •

"Despite what you may think," the psychiatrist said to his patient, "you do not have any kind of complex. The fact is, you *are* inferior."

• ■ •

"Dr. Gunj, you've got to help me. No one pays *any* attention to me."

"Next!"

• ■ •

"Well, Mr. Russell," said the psychiatrist, "I can state confidently that you're cured of the delusion that you're Elvis Presley."

"Great!" said the patient. "Can I call my wife Priscilla with the good news?"

• ▉ •

Mr. Avian settled down on the couch. "You've got to help me, doctor. I have this fondness for doing bird imitations."

"That doesn't seem so bad to me," the doctor replied.

"Oh, sure! That's because *you* don't have to swallow the worms!"

• ▉ •

"Bert," said the analyst during his visit to the asylum, "why are you digging around in the mud?"

"It rained four inches and a quarter last night," said Bert.

"So?"

"Maybe I'll get lucky and find the quarter," Bert said.

• ▉ •

"Doctor," said Charles, "I can't stop thinking I'm a suspension bridge!"

"Good lord, Charles, what's come over you?"

"So far, two trucks, five cars, and a bus."

• ◼ •

"Occasionally, I experience a complete and utter loss of memory," Tracy said to the psychiatrist. "What do you recommend?"

The doctor said, "Pay me in advance."

• ◼ •

"You've got to do something about my short-term memory," Gregory told his analyst. "I don't seem to *have* any."

"I'll do what I can. How long have you had this problem?"

Gregory gave him a quizzical look. "What problem?"

• ◼ •

"So," said the analyst, "you say you've got this problem with making up your mind."

"Well, yes and no—"

• ◼ •

"Doctor," said George, "is it possible for a human being to be passionately in love with an octopus?"

"No, and I urge you to rid yourself of this obsession."

"Okay," said George. "By the way, do you know anyone who might want to buy eight engagement rings?"

• ■ •

"I know it's crazy," Melvin said to his shrink, "but I can't stop thinking I'm a package of saltines."

"I see," said the analyst. "Let's see if we can convince you that you're not crackers."

• ■ •

The psychiatrist's receptionist quit her job in a huff.

"I just couldn't win," she told a friend. "If I was early, I had an anxiety complex. If I was late, I was hostile. And if I was on time, I was compulsive!"

• ■ •

The man walked into the analyst's office and shoved a wad of tobacco up his nose.

"Hmmm," said the psychiatrist, "you've certainly come to the right place."

"Why?" said the man. "You got a light?"

• ■ •

Q: What did the psychiatrist tell the man who thought his head was a drum?
A: "Beat it!"

• ■ •

Wilson sat down at the counter in the diner, ordered a Coke, lifted the glass, and poured it all over the floor.

"I'm *so* ashamed," he said to the waitress. "I always do that—and I'm always ashamed of myself right after."

Instead of getting angry, the waitress said, "You know, my sister had a crazy habit like that. She went to see this guy in town, Dr. Young, and he cured her. You oughta go see him."

Wilson thanked her and took her advice. A month later, he came back to the diner and ordered a Coke. As the waitress watched, Wilson picked the glass up and spilled the contents all over the floor.

"I guess you didn't see Dr. Young," she said.

"On the contrary," Wilson said.

"I guess he didn't do you any good."

"Wrong again."

"But you just spilled the Coke on the floor."

"Right," said Wilson, "only now I'm not the least bit ashamed!"

•　■　•

"Dr. Amana, I can't stop thinking I'm a refrigerator."

"I see. Does this disturb you?"

"Not really—"

"Then I wouldn't worry about it."

"But Dr. Amana, I sleep with my mouth open."

"So?"

"The light keeps my wife awake."

•　■　•

"So tell me," the woman said to the psychiatrist, "have you discovered why my husband flies off the handle so much?"

The analyst replied, "Yes. He's got a screw loose."

•　■　•

"Doctor," said the young man, "I've got this bizarre feeling that sometimes I'm a teepee and the rest of the time I'm a wigwam. What's wrong with me?"

"You're two tents."

•　■　•

"I just don't know what to do," Wesley told his shrink. "There's something *eating* at my mind."

"I wouldn't worry about it," said the psychiatrist. "It's bound to starve to death."

• ◼ •

"Dr. Hess," said Barbara, "I'm not here for myself but for a friend. She thinks she's an owl!"

"Who?"

"My god, now there are *two* of you!"

• ◼ •

"Doctor," said Stu, "I'm a kleptomaniac."

"I see. Are you taking anything for it?"

• ◼ •

"Do you really think you've cured my kleptomania?" Stu asked after dozens of sessions.

"Absolutely," said the doctor. "And to prove it, I want you to go down the street to Computer Universe and walk all through the store."

"I'll do it," Stu said.

"Just one thing," said the doctor. "If you

do have a relapse, I could use a second disc drive."

• ■ •

"You've been here an hour," the psychiatrist said to his newest patient, "and there's one thing I definitely want you to do before our next session. Give up smoking."

"Will that help me?" the patient asked.

"No, me. You've already burned two holes in my couch."

• ■ •

"Psychiatry has worked *wonders* for me!" Chuck enthused to a friend. "Why, last year, whenever the doorbell rang, I refused to answer it. Today, I answer it whether it rings or not!"

• ■ •

"Doctor," Dean whined, "it's just *awful*. I can see into the future! I know *everything* that's going to happen!"

"I see. When did this problem start?"

"Next Monday."

• ■ •

Then there was the psychiatrist who said to his ultra-inhibited patient, "Your problem is that you're tied up in nots . . ."

• ■ •

. . . and the psychiatrist who was always giving fee advice . . .

• ◀ •

. . . and the analyst who billed himself as a trauma critic.

• ■ •

"Doctor, you've got to do something," said Harvey.

"What's the problem?"

"I can't help thinking I'm a horse."

"Hmmm . . . I can cure you, but it'll take time *and* it will be expensive."

"Money's no object," said Harvey. "I just won the Preakness."

• ■ •

"Help me!" Ziggy screamed. "I feel like I'm a pot of boiling water!"

"Just simmer down," the shrink said.

● ◼ ●

"It's just *awful!*" Roderick wept. "I—I wake up each morning and fancy that I'm a pair of curtains!"

"Listen," said the doctor, "you've got to pull yourself together."

● ◼ ●

"Doctor," Jose whimpered, "I think I'm losing my mind!"

"Look on the bright side," said the doctor. "You won't miss it."

● ◼ ●

Kenneth said to the doctor, "I'm here, sir, because I like pie and my family thinks I'm crazy."

"That doesn't sound so crazy. I like pie too."

"You do?" beamed Kenneth. "Then you must come over and see mine. I've got over five thousand of them."

● ◼ ●

Then there was the psychiatrist who put his nymphomaniac patient on a strict diet, just three males a day . . .

• ■ •

. . . and the psychiatrist who was thrown out of a bar when the proprietor learned he was too Jung . . .

• ■ •

. . . and the other psychiatrist who had long ago concluded that life is just a bed of neuroses . . .

• ■ •

. . . and the analyst who had a sectional for treating people with split personalities . . .

• ■ •

. . . and one mustn't forget the hip psychiatrist who described himself as a Freudy cat.

• ■ •

The woman called her psychiatrist in a tizzy. "I had the *worst* dream last night!"
"Tell me about it."
"I dreamed I was walking down the street wearing nothing but a hat and a handbag."

"That *is* terrible," the psychiatrist said.
"Oh, it was just awful. They didn't match!"

• ■ •

"I've stopped seeing my analyst," Jessica said to Walter. "He had the nerve to say that I was in love with my computer."
"How ridiculous."
"I mean, we're really *fond* of each other—but love?"

• ◀ •

"Doc," said Terri, "I feel schizophrenic.
"That makes four of us," said the doctor.

• ■ •

The fighter pilot was being examined for a Section Eight discharge.
"I don't understand it," said the psychiatrist. "Your tail gunner told you to watch out for enemies at nine o'clock, yet you took no evasive action. Why?"
"What was the point? It was only eight forty-five."

• ■ •

The psychiatrist showed up for the convention only to learn that there were no rooms left in the hotel.

"Listen," said the psychiatrist, "if the President of the United States walked in the door, you'd find a room for him, wouldn't you?"

"Yes, we would," said the woman at the desk.

"Fine. He's not coming, so I'll take his room."

•   ■   •

"Dr. Kidd," said Arnie, "I have the strangest feeling that I'm covered with gold paint."

"Don't worry about it. That's just your gilt complex."

•   ■   •

Then there was the nymphomaniac who paid her psychiatrist in advances . . .

•   ■   •

. . . and the psychiatrist who pointed out that his was the only business in which the customer is always wrong.

● ■ ●

"What are you prescribing for me?" Dove asked the psychiatrist.

"Chocolate."

"Why?"

The doctor said, "Because you're nuts."

● ■ ●

Daft Danielle showed up outside her psychiatrist's apartment, which was also in her building.

"What are you doing here?" he said. "It's Sunday."

"I know, Dr. Tendler, but I'm making this cake and the recipe said to put an egg in a bowl and beat it for ten minutes."

"So?"

"I had nowhere else to go."

● ■ ●

"Congratulations," the psychiatrist said to Stephen. "You're cured."

"Big deal!" Stephen complained. "Before I came to you I was Abraham Lincoln. Now I'm nobody!"

● ■ ●

"I'm beginning to understand the source of your problem," the psychiatrist said to her patient. "Tell me: why do you hate your mother?"

"I don't," said the patient. "In fact, I love my mother very, very much."

"Look," the doctor snapped, "if you're not going to cooperate, I'll never be able to help you."

• ■ •

The psychiatrist was driving through the snowy countryside when he saw an old man, buck naked, chopping wood. Curious, the analyst pulled up beside the man and rolled down his window.

"Excuse me, sir, but you *do* know that it's below freezing, and it's a bad idea to do what you're doing."

"Maybe," said the old man, "but I've been getting dressed by a roarin' fire for sixty-two years, and I ain't about to stop now."

• ■ •

Then there was the psychiatrist who was able to build himself a new house thanks to mental blocks . . .

• ■ •

. . . while another one was able to build his new house using mad money.

• ■ •

"I feel like a new man," the schizophrenic patient said after years of treatment.

"Anyone I know?" asked his doctor.

• ■ •

The phone and doorbell both rang while Will was on the couch.

"Will, would you answer the door?" the psychiatrist said as he answered the phone.

Will got up and said, "Hello, door."

• ■ •

Bernadette called the psychiatrist. "You've got to do something about my sister Brigitte."

"You mean the beauty contest winner?"

"That's right," said Bernadette. "She's sitting in front of the TV with nothing on."

The psychiatrist's heart began to throb, and he broke a longstanding tradition about not making house calls. Before leaving, he phoned several of his colleagues, inviting them all to come along for second, third, and fourth opinions.

Shattering the speed limit and very nearly the sound barrier, the men drove to the house and ran to the front door. When Bernadette opened the door, they piled past her and rushed into the living room.

And every male heart in the room sank: the TV screen was blank.

• ■ •

Then there was the psychiatrist who didn't charge her patient full price because he was fifty percent off . . .

• ■ •

. . . and the transvestite who told his analyst that when he died he wanted to be buried abroad . . .

• ■ •

. . . and the psychiatrist who received a postcard from one of his patients. It read, "Having a wonderful time. Why?"

• ■ •

Docksteader said to his shrink, "You should be proud of me. I had a gas leak in my apartment and I fixed it all by myself."

"I *am* proud. How did you do it?"

"I didn't pay the bill for three months and they shut it off."

• ■ •

Louis told the psychiatrist, "My problem is that I yearn for my freewheeling youth. I guess my fondest memory is when I was a teenager and lived on nothing but salt water for two weeks."

"That's not possible," said the shrink.

"Sure it is. I did it."

"When was this?" the doctor asked dubiously.

Louis replied, "When I took a cruise to England."

• ■ •

Then there was also the psychiatrist who specialized in psychoceramics, the study of crackpots . . .

• ■ •

. . . and the psychiatrist who had two baskets on his desk, one labled *outgoing*, the other *inhibited*.

• ■ •

Lovely Lois came to see Dr. Hoople for her first session. When the curvaceous lass walked in, the doctor told her to undress and lie on the couch. After Lois had done so, the doctor pulled off his own clothes, threw himself on top of her, and made frenzied love to the woman.

When he was finished, Dr. Hoople said, "Well, that takes care of my problem. Now—what's yours?"

• ■ •

Then there was the man who went to the psychiatrist for help with his multiple personalities. The doctor was kind enough to give him a group rate.

• ■ •

"You know why my wife sent me to see you?" Sol asked the doctor. "Because we went out to a Japanese restaurant and I ate my dinner raw."

"Why, that's hardly unusual. I often do that myself."

"Really?" Sol asked. "And do you go to the movies naked too?"

• ■ •

Marci said to her psychiatrist, "I've got this irrational fear that I won't hear my crippled old mother if she falls out of bed. What should I do?"

"Take out the carpet," the doctor suggested.

• ■ •

Then there was the psychiatrist who described herself as someone who finds out what makes a person tick before they explode . . .

• ■ •

. . . another psychiatrist who said that his couch was a place where people ended up when they were off their rocker . . .

• ■ •

. . . and the patient who described himself as someone who went to the psychiatrist slightly cracked and came away completely broke.

• ■ •

That same patient said he went to the psychiatrist in search of mental balance and ended up with no bank balance . . .

• ■ •

. . . and who described his psychiatrist as a shrink because that's what the man did to his wallet.

• ■ •

"People can't take my delusions of grandeur," the patient said. "They've ostracized me, refuse to have anything to do with me."

"That's a shame. But you know—it would help more if you were to start at the beginning."

"Fine," said the patient, settling back on the couch. "In the beginning, I created the heavens and the earth. . . ."

• ■ •

"I'm really at the end of my wits," said Mrs. Boone. "Every single time I get into my car, I have an accident."

"I hate to ask," said the psychiatrist, "but you *do* stay on your side of the road, don't you? You understand that's what the white line's for."

Mrs. Boone's eyes widened. "You mean, that's not for bicycles?"

• ■ •

"You're just tense," the analyst said to Mr. Wengler. "If I were you, I'd go home, take my wife to the movies, and try to forget everything else."

"Y'know, I think I'll do that," he said. "What's your home number?"

• ■ •

The psychiatrist said to his receptionist, "Ah . . . there goes the only woman I've ever loved."

"Ms. Adler?" she said. "So why don't you marry her."

"Can't afford to," he said. "She's my best patient."

• ■ •

Then there was the nutrition-conscious psychiatrist who founded an asylum which served soup to nuts . . .

• ◼ •

. . . and the shrink who specialized in curing insomnia. He called it the triumph of mind over mattress.

• ◼ •

"I'm concerned," the woman said to her shrink. "I found my daughter and the little boy next door stark naked, examining each other's privates."

"That's perfectly natural," said the psychiatrist. "I wouldn't lose any sleep over it."

"But I *can't* stop worrying," the woman said, "and neither can my son-in-law."

• ◼ •

Essex bumped into Gloucester outside the psychiatrist's office.

"Fancy meeting you here!" said Essex. "Are you coming or going?"

Gloucester replied, "If I knew that, my good man, I wouldn't be here."

• ■ •

Then there was the psychiatrist who made a study of men who underwent sex change operations. He found they all had a common condition which he called their Addapuss Complex . . .

• ■ •

Q: According to psychiatrists, what's the difference between a young male athlete and a lunatic?
A: One's the flower of manhood, the other's a blooming idiot.

• ■ •

The man led his wife into the psychiatrist's office.

"What seems to be the problem?" the doctor asked.

"My husband doesn't give me any attention," the woman sobbed.

The man snorted. "What's-her-name doesn't know what she's talking about!"

• ■ •

Mr. Petty went to see Dr. Wells at the suggestion of his wife. To learn a little about his new patient, the doctor used a variation of the Rorschach test: he lay a stack of index cards on the desk before him. There was a "W" written on the top card.

"What does this remind you of?" the doctor asked.

The man said, "Tits."

Dr. Wells put it aside, exposing a card with a "V."

"And this?"

"A pussy."

Dr. Wells set out a third card. This one had a "P" on it.

"That's a side view of a babe," said Petty.

Dr. Wells said, "Your problem, Mr. Petty, is very clear: you're obsessed with sex."

"Me?" said Mr. Petty. "Christ, man, *you're* the one with the dirty picture collection!"

●　■　●

Finally, there was the wag who described his psychiatrist as someone you visit when you're going crazy, and who helps you . . .

• ■ •

. . . and the psychiatrist who stopped listening to a patient because she started making sense. . . .

• ■ •

SPECIALISTS

What do you call a doctor who . . .

. . . thinks Alka-Seltzer is a cure-all? A fizzician.

. . . doesn't make much money treating feet? A po'diatrist.

. . . steadies himself with rope? A guynecologist.

. . . examines kangaroos? An hoptometrist.

. . . puts on a Japanese sash when it's time to deliver babies? An obistetrician.

. . . takes care of former soldiers? A veteranarian.

. . . only treats skin diseases of elephants? A pachydermatologist.

. . . examines broken automobiles? A caroner.

. . . works for Daddy Warbucks? An anniethesiologist.

. . . has been knighted? A sirgeon.

. . . recently performed her first brain operation? A newrosurgeon.

. . . hails from Egypt? A Cairopractor.

. . . has eight arms? A doctopus.

• ■ •

"Doctor," said James, "how can I keep from getting a blinding pain in my eye whenever I drink coffee?"

The ophthalmologist replied, "Take the spoon out of the cup."

• ■ •

"Doctor," Smith asked his chiropractor, "why is my back stiff as a board?"

"Have you forgotten?" the doctor replied. "That's your lumbar region."

• ■ •

It was her first trip to the gynecologist, and lovely Peggy Sue was embarrassed.

"There's no reason to be," the doctor assured her.

"I know . . . but do you mind if I undress in that closet over there?"

"Not at all," said the doctor.

When she was finished, the young woman asked, "Where shall I put my clothes?"

The doctor said, "Right here, next to mine."

As the X-ray technician walked down the aisle with a former patient, one usher said to another, "I wonder what she saw in him?"

Then there was the X-ray technician who worked for a podiatrist and specialized in footographs . . .

. . . and the fertility specialist who took eggsrays . . .

. . . and the technician who only took pictures of people who had lost weight. He called them ex-weighs.

After the beautiful young dancer twisted her chronically weak ankle for the third time in as many weeks, the chiropodist said, "I just don't understand what a joint like this is doing in a nice girl like you."

• ■ •

Then there was the internist who had inside information . . .

• ■ •

. . . and the gynecologist who delighted in calling himself a privates investigator. . . .

• ■ •

Q: What's the difference between someone who picks up the tab and a chiropodist?
A: One foots the bill, the other does the opposite.

• ■ •

"Hmmmm," said the optometrist, "I think you need glasses."
"But I'm already wearing them," said the patient.
"Hmmmm," said the optometrist, "I think I need glasses."

• ■ •

Before operating on the woman, the plastic surgeon said to her husband, "I'm going to give your wife a local anesthetic."

"I want her to have the best," said the man. "Make it imported."

• ■ •

Q: What's the difference between a busybody and a proctologist?

A: One butts in, the other's in butts.

• ■ •

Rod said to Mary, "I hear your sister went to a modeling agency and got several offers."

"Yes," said Mary. "From plastic surgeons."

• ■ •

Corey was sitting on the examining table in the proctologist's office.

"Tell me," said the doctor, "did you see anyone else before coming to me with this problem?"

"Yes, sir," said Corey. "I went to see my GP, Dr. Horn."

"*That* quack!" the proctologist cried. "And what did the idiot tell you?"

"To come and see you."

• ■ •

Then there was the pundit who pointed out that specialists are people who know more and more about less and less. . . .

• ■ •

Ms. D'Artagnon, a single woman, went to a fertility specialist for artificial insemination. Unfortunately, when she arrived she learned from Dr. Hauser that the sperm she'd selected from a deceased genius had been used for another recipient.

"Damn," she said. "What am I going to do now?"

"Well," said Dr. Hauser, unzipping his fly, "since we're out of the bottled goods, we might as well use draft."

• ■ •

Then there was the fertility specialist who found that babies conceived through artificial insemination tend to be scrawnier than those conceived in the usual fashion. His conclusion: spare the rod and spoil the child.

• ■ •

Jan told Joe, "I was seeing spots before my eyes, so I went to an ophthalmologist. She gave me glasses."

"Did that help?"

"Yes, indeed. The spots are much clearer now."

• ■ •

Joe said to Jan, "You mean, your eyes were never checked before that?"

"No," she said. "They've always been solid blue."

• ■ •

Then there was cross-eyed Irma, who went to the eye doctor. Seems she'd tried to kill her husband with a look and killed another man instead.

• ■ •

The obstetrician said to Mrs. Rank, "I hate to say this, but your daughter has a venereal disease."

"How is that *possible*?" the woman gasped. "Could she have gotten it on a toilet seat?"

"Perhaps," said the doctor, "but that would have been mighty uncomfortable."

• ■ •

Then there was the urologist who didn't bother to advertise: no sooner did he hang up his shingle than people came trickling in.

• ■ •

Q: What's the difference between a teacher and an optometrist?
A: Nothing. They both look at pupils.

• ■ •

C.B. asked the eye doctor, "What'll happen if I sleep in my contact lenses?"

The doctor replied, "Your feet will stick out."

• ■ •

Elderly Mr. Caine and Mr. Reeve were sitting on the park bench.

"You really ought to see my urologist,"

said Mr. Caine. "He's marvelous. The best."

"But there's nothing wrong with me," Mr. Reeve said.

"Tish tosh. My doctor is so good he'll *find* something!"

• ■ •

Q: What's the difference between a religious vision and having blood drawn?
A: Nothing. Both are holy experiences.

• ■ •

Mrs. Derrick went to the eye doctor because she was having trouble with her eyes.

"Let's see if we can find out what the problem is," the doctor said. He stood beside an eye chart. "What am I pointing at?"

"I—I can't see," the woman said.

He pointed to the window. "What am I pointing at now?"

"I have no idea," she replied.

Suddenly, he whipped out his private member and pointed to it. "How about now?"

"You're pointing to your genitals," she said.

"That's your problem," he said triumphantly. "You're cockeyed!"

• ■ •

Mabel said to Blanche, "I just saw the ear, nose, and throat man and he gave me a hearing aid."
"Did he? And how does it work?"
"Dr. Schwartz," she replied.

• ■ •

Then there was the orthopedist who got all the breaks . . .

• ■ •

. . . and the Olympic athlete who went to a chiropractor after suffering a slipped discus . . .

• ■ •

. . . and the optometrist who moved to Alaska and became an optical Aleutian.

• ■ •

Finally, there was the doctor who worked so hard to specialize in every form of medicine that he ended up killing himself by degrees.

• ■ •

"Hi, doctor," said Henry.

"Bet you're here for new glasses," the optometrist said.

"You haven't even examined me!" said Henry.

"I know, but that's the gum machine you just greeted."

• ■ •

The old obstetrician said to Craig, "When your grandfather was born, they passed out cigars. And when your dad was born, they passed out cigars."

"Did they pass out cigars when I was born?" Craig asked.

The doctor said, "Well—you're partly right."

• ■ •

Then there was the busy gynecologist whose office had standing womb only . . .

• ■ •

. . . and the fertility specialist who had the unpleasant task of informing the elderly gentleman that he was not heir-conditioned.

• ■ •

As the fertility expert put it to another impotent old man, "The spurt is willing, but the flesh is weak."

• ■ •

Dr. Frank had performed a delicate eye operation and restored the vision of a famous painter. In a gesture of thanksgiving, the artist presented Dr. Frank with a canvas—a portrait of the ophthalmologist inside a giant eyeball.

Dr. Frank brought the painting home and showed it to his wife.

"What do you think?" he asked.

After studying it long and hard, Mrs. Frank said, "I'm very glad I didn't marry a proctologist."

• ■ •

Then there was the very stuffy pharmacist whose motto was, "We dispense with formality . . ."

• ■ •

. . . and the optometrists who opened offices called, *A Sight for Sore Eyes*. . .

• ■ •

. . . and the dermatologist who made rash promises . . .

• ■ •

. . . and the sex therapist who specialized in treating frigid women. Seems he found a way to lick the problem.

• ■ •

"How much will it cost to make my nose smaller," Diana asked the plastic surgeon.

"Four thousand dollars."

"That's a lot," she said. "Can you suggest anything cheaper?"

"Sure," he said. "Run into a brick wall."

• ■ •

Q: What's the difference between a prophet and a proctologist?

A: One sees ahead, the other behind.

• ■ •

"I'm working myself to death," Minton told the doctor.

"Why'd you come to me?" said the doctor. "I'm an ophthalmologist."

"Because I'm nearsighted. I can never tell when the boss is watching."

• ■ •

Dumb Donna started when the gynecologist entered the examination room.

"I'm sorry," he smiled. "Did I take you unaware?"

She glanced at her clothing, which was piled on a chair. "No. They're still there."

• ■ •

Then there was the plastic surgeon who wasn't able to take people at face value . . .

• ■ •

. . . and the woman who was going to have her face lifted until she found out what it would cost. She just let the whole thing drop.

• ■ •

"I'll tell you this," Aaron said after leaving the allergist. "Her bill is nothing to sneeze at."

•   ■   •

Chiropractor Nelson said to wealthy Roger, "What can you *possibly* be here for? You press a button to summon the maid, press another button to turn on the home entertainment system, and press another to open the garage door. What on earth can be wrong with you?"

Roger said, "My finger hurts."

•   ■   •

The gynecologist poked his head into the examining room and asked Mrs. Talbot to remove all of her clothing. A few minutes later, he knocked and then entered.

After examining her thoroughly, he said, "You look to be in fine health. Do you have any questions?"

"Just one," she said. "Why on earth did you *knock*?"

•   ■   •

Q: What's the difference between a laborer and a gynecologist?

A: One's bushed at the end of the day, the other all day.

•　■　•

Then there was the man who became a specialist so he could have a smaller practice and a larger house . . .

•　■　•

. . . and the obstetrician who put himself through medical school by working in the post office. Now it takes him a week to deliver a baby.

•　■　•

"I don't understand," the optometrist said to young Lucy. "Why are you coming to *me* if you're pregnant?"

"Because," she said, "I just found out that those were M&Ms I was taking each morning."

•　■　•

Ms. Olivetti called her acupuncturist to complain about a pain in her arm.

The doctor said, "Take two safety pins and call me in the morning."

• ■ •

Mr. Monroe was walking by the wharf when he saw a man whistling as he rigged his own thirty-two foot sailboat.

"You seem a fit and happy fellow!" Mr. Monroe said.

"I am."

"Tell me—what's your secret?"

"Pills."

"You take *pills* to make you content?"

"No," the man said. "I sell them."

• ■ •

SURGEONS

Mr. Kahrs was somber as he entered the doctor's office. Dr. Iovino told him to take a seat.

"There's no doubt about it," said the surgeon, "you need this operation. But I'm obliged to inform you that it's a dangerous operation: two out of three patients don't survive."

"I see."

"But I wouldn't worry about it, Mr. Kahrs. You're sure to make it."

"Why?"

"Because my last two patients died."

• ■ •

As it happens, Mr. Kahrs didn't make it. In order to collect his fee, the surgeon logged his bill in probate court.

"Will I need this notarized?" the surgeon asked.

"That won't be necessary," said the clerk. "Mr. Kahrs's death is evidence enough that you rendered professional services."

• ■ •

Then there was the surgeon who referred to prostate operations as lowbotomies. . . .

• ■ •

After undergoing open-heart surgery, Bernie was told he must discontinue smoking, drinking, and eating fatty foods.

"What about sex?" he said. "Can I still do that?"

"Yes," said the doctor, "but only with your wife. I don't want you to become *too* excited."

• ■ •

The skinflint was sitting on the operating table counting out dollar bills.

"That's all right," said the surgeon. "You don't pay me until the work is finished."

"I don't intend to," said the miser. "I'm counting what I have before you put me under."

• ■ •

Q: What did the surgeon say to the patient after sewing her up?
A: That's enough out of you!"

• ■ •

"How'd the suturing go, Dr. Grimley?"
"Sew-sew," he answered.

• ■ •

Dr. Douglas met Dr. Lancaster in post-op.
"How'd Mr. Finster's tonsillectomy go?" asked Dr. Douglas.
"Tonsillectomy?" Lancaster said. "Christ, I thought it was an autopsy!"

• ■ •

The motorcyclist awoke and found himself in a hospital, a surgeon examining his leg.
"Doctor," said the biker, "what happened?"
"You were in an accident," said the doctor, "and I've got good news and bad news."
"What's the good news?" he asked.

"Well—the leg that was mangled in the accident is healing quite nicely."

"And what's the bad news?"

"I cut off your good leg by mistake."

• ■ •

Mr. Clark ran up to the surgeon, grabbed him by the lapels, and shouted, "Doc, you've got to help me! I was at the zoo and I just couldn't control myself! I opened my mouth real wide and swallowed an elephant!"

"That's not possible," the surgeon replied.

"It *is!*" screamed the man. "I *did* it!"

Seeking to put the disturbed man's mind at rest, the surgeon agreed to operate. After the man was asleep, the surgeon wheeled him to the parking lot and had the zoo bring an elephant over.

When the man awoke, the surgeon showed him the elephant.

"There," said the doctor. "I got it out in one piece."

The man glared at the surgeon. "What do you think I am, *stupid*? That's an African elephant! The one I swallowed was Indian!"

• ■ •

Then there was the surgeon who sent a woman screaming from the hospital dance when he asked, "May I cut in?"

• ■ •

. . . and the surgeon who sandpapered his fingers so he'd be a smooth operator . . .

• ■ •

. . . and another who charged cut-rate prices . . .

• ■ •

. . . yet another who was so timid he was afraid to open a conversation . . .

• ■ •

. . . still another who wore a tuxedo because he believed in formal openings . . .

• ■ •

. . . and one more who performed a special service for people who couldn't afford surgery: he retouched their X-rays.

• ■ •

"I'm nervous," the patient said to the doctor. "This is my first operation."

The doctor smiled. "I'm nervous too. It's also *my* first."

• ■ •

After her husband's third trip to the hospital for open-heart surgery, the doctor told Mrs. Blum that he'd need yet another operation.

Anguished and forlorn, the woman rose and said angrily, "You know, doctor, I'm sick and tired of people opening my male!"

• ■ •

Q: What did the surgeon say to her dissatisfied patient?
A: "Next time, suture self!"

• ■ •

"Perk up," the surgeon told his patient. "This operation you're going to have? I had the same one myself just a year ago."

"Yes," said the patient, "but you didn't have the same surgeon."

• ■ •

Dr. Hecht met Dr. Hill in the surgeons' lounge.

"I hear you operated on Mr. Williams last week," said Dr. Hecht.

"Did five thousand dollars worth of work," said Dr. Hill.

"What did he have?"

"Five thousand dollars," answered Dr. Hill.

• ■ •

"You don't have any medical insurance?" the surgeon said to Mr. Magillicutty with some distress.

"No, I don't."

"Okay, then here's what you do. Give me three thousand dollars up-front, and you can pay off the rest at five hundred dollars a month for twenty months."

"Just like buying a new car," said the patient.

"Actually, a boat," said the doctor.

• ■ •

Over a year later, Mr. Magillicutty said to his surgeon, "You've cut me open twice, I've given you over ten thousand dollars, and I'm *still* not better! What the hell kind of a surgeon are you, anyway?"

"A damn good one, you ungrateful wretch!" the surgeon said. "And to think, I named the yacht after you!"

• ■ •

Then there was the man who bought a surgeon doll that operated on batteries . . .

• ■ •

. . . the surgeon who didn't use sutures during open-heart surgery, he used ticker tape . . .

• ■ •

. . . and the surgeon who told a patient that if he didn't cut something out, he'd have to cut something out.

• ■ •

Q: What's the difference between a comedian and a surgeon?
A: Nothing. Both keep people in stitches.

• ■ •

The reporter from *The Medical World* was interviewing Myra Bluth, the world-famous brain surgeon.

"And what do you do between operations?" the reporter asked.

"I keep busy," Myra said. "I have three children."

"Each time?" the reporter asked.

• ■ •

After having her appendix removed, Ms. Quentin asked the surgeon, "Will the scar show?"

"That," the doctor replied, "is entirely up to you."

• ■ •

Upon waking up from surgery, Patterson was shocked to find himself in complete darkness.

"Nurse . . ." he rasped. "Nurse, I can't see anything."

He felt a reassuring pat on the shoulder. "Don't worry, Mr. Patterson. There's a fire in the building across the street, so I drew the blinds."

"Why?"

She said, "I didn't want you to think the operation had failed."

• ■ •

Then there was the little boy who swallowed a fork and spoon and had to have his utensils removed . . .

• ■ •

. . . and the obstetrician who told the new mother that there was no trick to raising a baby. "Just remember," he said, "always keep one end full and the other end empty."

• ■ •

BIG MOUTH, OR, "DOCTOR, I JUST SWALLOWED . . ."

Big Mouth screamed into the phone, "Doctor, I just swallowed a spoon! What should I do?"

"Don't stir," the doctor advised.

●　■　●

Later, Big Mouth called back. "Doctor, I just swallowed a role of film! What should I do?"

"Nothing," the doctor said. "Let's just see what develops."

●　■　●

Still eating what he shouldn't, Big Mouth swallowed a live frog, then called the doctor.

"People eat frogs all the time," the doctor said, "so don't worry."

"That's easy for you to say!" Big Mouth retorted. "I'm the one who could croak at any minute!"

•　■　•

The next day around breakfast time, Big Mouth shouted into the phone, "Doctor, I just swallowed a pen! What should I do?"

The doctor replied, "Use a pencil."

•　■　•

"I swallowed a doorknob and I feel like hell," Big Mouth complained shortly thereafter.

"What did you expect?" the doctor replied. "Something like that's certainly going to turn your stomach."

•　■　•

"Holy Hannah!" Big Mouth said to the doctor, "I just swallowed a bullet! What do you suggest?"

"Eat some beans and stand in front of your mother-in-law."

• ■ •

"Doctor!" Big Mouth gasped over the phone, "I just swallowed a bone."
"Are you choking?"
"No!" he wheezed. "I'm serious!"

• ■ •

Big Mouth yelled, "Doctor, I just swallowed some plutonium!"
"Then you'll almost certainly have atomic ache."

• ■ •

Big Mouth hollered, "Doctor, I just swallowed my harmonica! What should I do?"
"Get down on your knees and thank God you weren't playing a bassoon!"

• ■ •

"Doctor," Big Mouth complained, "yesterday I swallowed a clock!"
"Yesterday? Why didn't you call me then?"
Big Mouth said, "I didn't want to alarm you."

• ■ •

"Help me," Big Mouth implored. "I just swallowed a roll of quarters."

"Don't worry," said the doctor. "Stay in bed until you see some change."

• ■ •

"I just swallowed a deck of cards!" Big Mouth said in a panic.

"I'll deal with you later," the doctor told him.

• ■ •

This time, Big Mouth came to the office in person and cried, "Doc, I just ate a pogo stick!"

"Sit down, sit down, sit down."

• ■ •

"Dumb me!" Big Mouth told the doctor. "I just ate a copy of the newspaper! What do you suggest?"

"Eat a copy of *Reader's Digest* next."

• ■ •

"Woe is me," whined Big Mouth. "I just ate a Monopoly board. What should I do?"

"There's nothing you *can* do," said the doctor, "except wait until you pass Go."

• ◼ •

"Doctor, I just ate a copy of this book and it made me sick!" Big Mouth wheezed.

"What's the matter," said the doctor. "Can't you take a joke?"

• ◼ •

By the year 2000, 2 out of 3 Americans could be illiterate.

It's true.

Today, 75 million adults...about one American in three, can't read adequately. And by the year 2000, U.S. News & World Report envisions an America with a literacy rate of only 30%.

Before that America comes to be, you can stop it...by joining the fight against illiteracy today.

Call the Coalition for Literacy at toll-free **1-800-228-8813** and volunteer.

Volunteer Against Illiteracy. The only degree you need is a degree of caring.

THIS AD PRODUCED BY MARTIN LITHOGRAPHERS
A MARTIN COMMUNICATIONS COMPANY